Wonderful ways to prepare

FISH & SEAFOOD

by ANNETTE HALCOMB

OTHER TITLES IN THIS SERIES

Printed in Ca

Wonderful ways to prepare

FISH & SEAFOOD

PLAYMORE INC NEW YORK USA
UNDER ARRANGEMENT WITH
I. WALDMAN & SON INC

AYERS & JAMES PTY LTD
CROWS NEST AUSTRALIA

STAFFORD PEMBERTON PUBLISHING
KNUTSFORD UNITED KINGDOM

FIRST PUBLISHED 1978

PUBLISHED IN THE USA
BY PLAYMORE INC.
UNDER ARRANGEMENT WITH I. WALDMAN & SON INC.

PUBLISHED IN AUSTRALIA
BY AYERS & JAMES PTY. LTD.
CROWS NEST.   AUSTRALIA

PUBLISHED IN THE UNITED KINGDOM
BY STAFFORD PEMBERTON PUBLISHING
KNUTSFORD CHESIRE

COPYRIGHT © 1978
AYERS & JAMES PTY. LTD.
5 ALEXANDER STREET
CROWS NEST   N.S.W.   AUSTRALIA

ISBN 0 86908 057 1

OVEN TEMPERATURE GUIDE

Description	Gas		Electric		Mark
	C	F	C	F	
Cool	100	200	110	225	¼
Very Slow	120	250	120	250	½
Slow	150	300	150	300	1-2
Moderately slow	160	325	170	340	3
Moderate	180	350	200	400	4
Moderately hot	190	375	220	425	5-6
Hot	200	400	230	450	6-7
Very hot	230	450	250	475	8-9

LIQUID MEASURES

IMPERIAL	METRIC
1 teaspoon	5 ml
1 tablespoon	20 ml
2 fluid ounces (¼ cup)	62.5 ml
4 fluid ounces (½ cup)	125 ml
8 fluid ounces (1 cup)	250 ml
1 pint (16 ounces — 2 cups)*	500 ml

* (The imperial pint is equal to 20 fluid ounces.)

SOLID MEASURES

AVOIRDUPOIS	METRIC
1 ounce	30 g
4 ounces (¼ lb)	125 g
8 ounces (½ lb)	250 g
12 ounces (¾ lb)	375 g
16 ounces (1 lb)	500 g
24 ounces (1½ lb)	750 g
32 ounces (2 lb)	1000 g (1 kg)

CUP AND SPOON REPLACEMENTS FOR OUNCES

INGREDIENT	½ oz	1 oz	2 oz	3 oz	4 oz	5 oz	6 oz	7 oz	8 oz
Almonds, ground	2 T	¼ C	½ C	¾ C	1¼ C	1⅓ C	1⅔ C	2 C	2¼ C
slivered	6 t	¼ C	½ C	¾ C	1 C	1⅓ C	1⅔ C	2 C	2¼ C
whole	2 T	¼ C	⅓ C	½ C	¾ C	1 C	1¼ C	1⅓ C	1½ C
Apples, dried whole	3 T	½ C	1 C	1⅓ C	2 C	2⅓ C	2¾ C	3⅓ C	3¾ C
Apricots, chopped	2 T	¼ C	½ C	¾ C	1 C	1¼ C	1½ C	1¾ C	2 C
whole	2 T	3 T	½ C	⅔ C	1 C	1¼ C	1⅓ C	1½ C	1¾ C
Arrowroot	1 T	2 T	⅓ C	½ C	⅔ C	¾ C	1 C	1¼ C	1⅓ C
Baking Powder	1 T	2 T	⅓ C	½ C	⅔ C	¾ C	1 C	1 C	1¼ C
Baking Soda	1 T	2 T	⅓ C	½ C	⅔ C	¾ C	1 C	1 C	1¼ C
Barley	1 T	2 T	¼ C	½ C	⅔ C	¾ C	1 C	1 C	1¼ C
Breadcrumbs, dry	2 T	¼ C	½ C	¾ C	1 C	1¼ C	1½ C	1¾ C	2 C
soft	¼ C	½ C	1 C	1½ C	2 C	2½ C	3 C	3⅔ C	4¼ C
Biscuit Crumbs	2 T	¼ C	½ C	¾ C	1¼ C	1⅓ C	1⅔ C	2 C	2¼ C
Butter	3 t	6 t	¼ C	⅓ C	½ C	⅔ C	¾ C	1 C	1 C
Cheese, grated, lightly packed,									
natural cheddar	6 t	¼ C	½ C	¾ C	1 C	1¼ C	1½ C	1¾ C	2 C
Processed cheddar	5 t	2 T	⅓ C	⅔ C	¾ C	1 C	1¼ C	1½ C	1⅔ C
Parmesan, Romano	6 t	¼ C	½ C	¾ C	1 C	1⅓ C	1⅔ C	2 C	2¼ C
Cherries, candied, chopped	1 T	2 T	⅓ C	½ C	¾ C	1 C	1 C	1⅓ C	1½ C
whole	1 T	2 T	⅓ C	½ C	⅔ C	¾ C	1 C	1¼ C	1⅓ C
Cocoa	2 T	¼ C	½ C	¾ C	1¼ C	1⅓ C	1⅔ C	2 C	2¼ C
Coconut, desiccated	2 T	⅓ C	⅔ C	1 C	1⅓ C	1⅔ C	2 C	2⅓ C	2⅔ C
shredded	⅓ C	⅔ C	1¼ C	1¾ C	2½ C	3 C	3⅔ C	4⅓ C	5 C
Cornstarch	6 t	3 T	½ C	⅔ C	1 C	1¼ C	1½ C	1⅔ C	2 C
Corn Syrup	2 t	1 T	2 T	¼ C	⅓ C	½ C	½ C	⅔ C	⅔ C
Coffee, ground	2 T	⅓ C	⅔ C	1 C	1⅓ C	1⅔ C	2 C	2⅓ C	2⅔ C
instant	3 T	½ C	1 C	1⅓ C	1¾ C	2¼ C	2⅔ C	3 C	3½ C
Cornflakes	½ C	1 C	2 C	3 C	4¼ C	5¼ C	6¼ C	7⅓C	8⅓ C
Cream of Tartar	1 T	2 T	⅓ C	½ C	⅔ C	¾ C	1 C	1 C	1¼ C
Currants	1 T	2 T	⅓ C	⅔ C	¾ C	1 C	1¼ C	1½ C	1⅔ C
Custard Powder	6 t	3 T	½ C	⅔ C	1 C	1¼ C	1½ C	1⅔ C	2 C
Dates, chopped	1 T	2 T	⅓ C	⅔ C	¾ C	1 C	1¼ C	1½ C	1⅔ C
whole, pitted	1 T	2 T	⅓ C	½ C	¾ C	1 C	1¼ C	1⅓ C	1½ C
Figs, chopped	1 T	2 T	⅓ C	½ C	¾ C	1 C	1 C	1⅓ C	1½ C
Flour, all-purpose or cake	6 t	¼ C	½ C	¾ C	1 C	1¼ C	1½ C	1¾ C	2 C
wholemeal	6 t	3 T	½ C	⅔ C	1 C	1¼ C	1⅓ C	1⅔ C	1¾ C
Fruit, mixed	1 T	2 T	⅓ C	½ C	¾ C	1 C	1¼ C	1⅓ C	1½ C
Gelatine	5 t	2 T	⅓ C	½ C	¾ C	1 C	1 C	1¼ C	1½ C
Ginger, crystallised pieces	1 T	2 T	⅓ C	½ C	¾ C	1 C	1¼ C	1⅓ C	1½ C
ground	6 t	⅓ C	½ C	¾ C	1¼ C	1½ C	1¾ C	2 C	2¼ C
preserved, heavy syrup	1 T	2 T	⅓ C	½ C	⅔ C	¾ C	1 C	1 C	1¼ C
Glucose, liquid	2 t	1 T	2 T	¼ C	⅓ C	½ C	½ C	⅔ C	⅔ C
Haricot Beans	1 T	2 T	⅓ C	½ C	⅔ C	¾ C	1 C	1 C	1¼ C

In this table, t represents teaspoonful, T represents tablespoonful and C represents cupful.

CUP AND SPOON REPLACEMENTS FOR OUNCES (Cont.)

INGREDIENT	½ oz	1 oz	2 oz	3 oz	4 oz	5 oz	6 oz	7 oz	8 oz
Honey	2 t	1 T	2 T	¼ C	⅓ C	½ C	½ C	⅔ C	⅔ C
Jam	2 t	1 T	2 T	¼ C	⅓ C	½ C	½ C	⅔ C	¾ C
Lentils	1 T	2 T	⅓ C	½ C	⅔ C	¾ C	1 C	1 C	1¼ C
Macaroni (see pasta)									
Milk Powder, full cream	2 T	¼ C	½ C	¾ C	1¼ C	1⅓ C	1⅔ C	2 C	2¼ C
non fat	2 T	⅓ C	¾ C	1¼ C	1½ C	2 C	2⅓ C	2¾ C	3¼ C
Nutmeg	6 t	3 T	½ C	⅔ C	¾ C	1 C	1¼ C	1½ C	1⅔ C
Nuts, chopped	6 t	¼ C	½ C	¾ C	1 C	1¼ C	1½ C	1¾ C	2 C
Oatmeal	1 T	2 T	½ C	⅔ C	¾ C	1 C	1¼ C	1½ C	1⅔ C
Olives, whole	1 T	2 T	⅓ C	⅔ C	¾ C	1 C	1¼ C	1½ C	1⅔ C
sliced	1 T	2 T	⅓ C	⅔ C	¾ C	1 C	1¼ C	1½ C	1⅔ C
Pasta, short (e.g. macaroni)	1 T	2 T	⅓ C	⅔ C	¾ C	1 C	1¼ C	1½ C	1⅔ C
Peaches, dried & whole	1 T	2 T	⅓ C	⅔ C	¾ C	1 C	1¼ C	1½ C	1⅔ C
chopped	6 t	¼ C	½ C	¾ C	1 C	1¼ C	1½ C	1¾ C	2 C
Peanuts, shelled, raw, whole	1 T	2 T	⅓ C	½ C	¾ C	1 C	1¼ C	1⅓ C	1½ C
roasted	1 T	2 T	⅓ C	⅔ C	¾ C	1 C	1¼ C	1½ C	1⅔ C
Peanut Butter	3 t	6 t	3 T	⅓ C	½ C	½ C	⅔ C	¾ C	1 C
Peas, split	1 T	2 T	⅓ C	½ C	⅔ C	¾ C	1 C	1 C	1¼ C
Peel, mixed	1 T	2 T	⅓ C	½ C	¾ C	1 C	1 C	1¼ C	1½ C
Potato, powder	1 T	2 T	¼ C	⅓ C	½ C	⅔ C	¾ C	1 C	1¼ C
flakes	¼ C	½ C	1 C	1⅓ C	2 C	2⅓ C	2¾ C	3⅓ C	3¾ C
Prunes, chopped	1 T	2 T	⅓ C	½ C	⅔ C	¾ C	1 C	1¼ C	1⅓ C
whole pitted	1 T	2 T	⅓ C	½ C	⅔ C	¾ C	1 C	1 C	1¼ C
Raisins	2 T	¼ C	⅓ C	½ C	¾ C	1 C	1 C	1⅓ C	1½ C
Rice, short grain, raw	1 T	2 T	¼ C	½ C	⅔ C	¾ C	1 C	1 C	1¼ C
long grain, raw	1 T	2 T	⅓ C	½ C	¾ C	1 C	1¼ C	1⅓ C	1½ C
Rice Bubbles	⅔ C	1¼ C	2½ C	3⅔ C	5 C	6¼ C	7½ C	8¾ C	10 C
Rolled Oats	2 T	⅓ C	⅔ C	1 C	1⅓ C	1¾ C	2 C	2½ C	2¾ C
Sago	2 T	¼ C	⅓ C	½ C	¾ C	1 C	1 C	1¼ C	1½ C
Salt, common	3 t	6 t	¼ C	⅓ C	½ C	⅔ C	¾ C	1 C	1 C
Semolina	1 T	2 T	⅓ C	½ C	¾ C	1 C	1 C	1⅓ C	1½ C
Spices	6 t	3 T	¼ C	⅓ C	½ C	½ C	⅔ C	¾ C	1 C
Sugar, plain	3 t	6 t	¼ C	⅓ C	½ C	⅔ C	¾ C	1 C	1 C
confectioners'	1 T	2 T	⅓ C	½ C	¾ C	1 C	1 C	1¼ C	1½ C
moist brown	1 T	2 T	⅓ C	½ C	¾ C	1 C	1 C	1⅓ C	1½ C
Tapioca	1 T	2 T	⅓ C	½ C	⅔ C	¾ C	1 C	1¼ C	1⅓ C
Treacle	2 t	1 T	2 T	¼ C	⅓ C	½ C	½ C	⅔ C	⅔ C
Walnuts, chopped	2 T	¼ C	½ C	¾ C	1 C	1¼ C	1½ C	1¾ C	2 C
halved	2 T	⅓ C	⅔ C	1 C	1¼ C	1½ C	1¾ C	2¼ C	2½ C
Yeast, dried	6 t	3 T	½ C	⅔ C	1 C	1¼ C	1⅓ C	1⅔ C	1¾ C
compressed	3 t	6 t	3 T	⅓ C	½ C	½ C	⅔ C	¾ C	1 C

In this table, t represents teaspoonful, T represents tablespoonful and C represents cupful.

Contents

Hors d'œuvres and First Courses

East India Fish Soup

1½ lbs (750 g) flounder or sole
2 onions, sliced
2 large potatoes, sliced
10 oz (300 ml) milk
1 chicken stock cube
salt
2½ cups thick cream
½ teaspoon saffron
tumeric
freshly ground black pepper

1. Put sliced onions and potatoes with the milk and chicken stock cube and cook until potatoes are soft. Blend in an electric blender.
2. Poach the fish in salted water until just tender. Drain and remove bones and keep warm.
3. Put the blended mixture over a low heat and add cream and saffron and tumeric and bring to boil. Add the pieces of fish and season again if necessary.

Serves 4.

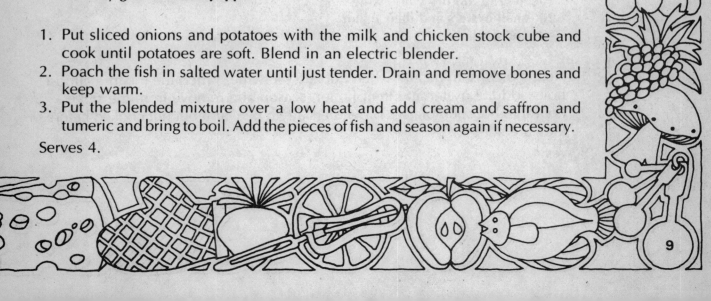

Iced Turtle Soup

2 tablespoons (15 g) gelatin
1 large can (500 ml or 16 oz)
   clear turtle soup
¾ can of water
dry sherry
lemon juice
sour cream
caviar

1. Dissolve the gelatin in a little cold water and mix with the turtle soup.
2. Using the empty can, fill with ¾ water and top with equal quantities of dry sherry and lemon juice. Season to taste and chill in a bowl until set.
3. Spoon into serving cups and garnish with a dot of sour cream and a sprinkle of caviar.

Serves 4.

Oyster Soup

3 cups (750 ml) rich chicken
   consomme
1 cup (250 ml) dry white wine
20 small oysters and their liquor
salt and pepper

1. Heat the consomme and when hot add the wine. When the mixture almost boils add the oyster and their liquor, season and remove from the stove.
2. Pour into hot soup plates. The oysters are to be warm but not cooked before they are added.

Serves 4.

Smoked Oyster Soup

1 can smoked oysters
1 can oyster soup
1 can of milk
salt and pepper
1½ cups cream
1 tablespoon dry sherry

Finely chop the oysters and put them in a saucepan. Add the oyster soup, place over heat until the mixture is smooth. Add 1 can of milk using the empty soup can as a measure. Season to taste and heat again slowly. Do not boil. Remove from the heat and stir in the cream and sherry. Heat again but do not boil and serve immediately.

A dot of sour cream sprinkled with parsley is a nice addition when serving the soup.

Serves 4.

Crab, Pea and Tomato Soup

1 lb (500 g) fresh peas
2 white onions, chopped
2 tablespoons (40 g) butter
2 cups (500 ml) milk
1¼ cups tomato purée
2 tablespoons (40 g) butter

6 oz (185 g) can crab meat
   or 8 oz (250 g) fresh
   crabmeat
basil
1 cup cream, scalded
2 tablespoons sherry

1. Saute the onions in the butter, add the peas and a very little water and cook until tender. Purée or blend in a blender with the milk.
2. Simmer the tomato purée for 4 minutes and put aside.
3. Heat the flaked crabmeat a few minutes in more butter in the top part of a double boiler.
4. Combine all ingredients and add the scalded cream and sherry and season with salt and pepper.

This soup can be made with lobster too.

Serves 4-6.

Crab and Shrimp Soup

½ lb (250 g) fish for stock
1 lb (500 g) shrimp cooked
2 bay leaves
2 cloves garlic, crushed
salt and pepper
1½ cups (375 ml) water
1 cup fresh or canned crabmeat
4 tablespoons (80 g) butter
½ cup chopped celery and leaves
2 cups (500 ml) milk

1 tablespoon flour
¼ teaspoon nutmeg
½ teaspoon marjoram
½ teaspoon thyme
2 tablespoons chilli sauce
1 tablespoon brown sugar
1 cup cream
2 egg yolks
¼ cup Madeira or sherry

1. Put the fish, bay leaves, cloves, salt and pepper in the water and cook slowly for 30 minutes. Let the fish cool in the broth, strain it and reserve the broth.
2. Peel the shrimp and remove all the bones from the fish and put them through the blender with a little of the stock.
3. Flake the crabmeat and add it to the other fish.
4. Sauté the onion and celery in the butter for 3 to 4 minutes, add the milk and simmer for 5 minutes. Mash through a sieve or blend and mix in the flour, add the other seasonings and combine with the fish and broth.
5. Thin with hot milk if necessary.
6. Just before serving boil up the soup, scald the cream and pour it over the beaten egg yolks and combine the mixture slowly. Check the seasoning, add the wine and serve.

Serves 4-6.

Clam Chowder

3 or 4 dozen clams (mussels
   can be used instead)
6 cups water
½ lb (250 g) bacon, chopped
5 onions, chopped
½ cup chopped celery
½ cup carrots, chopped
1 can tomato puree
   or 3 tomatoes skinned, seeded
   and chopped

2 cups cubed potatoes
salt and pepper
1 teaspoon thyme
dash Worcestershire sauce
2 bay leaves
2 tablespoons plain flour
2 tablespoons (40 g) butter
cayenne pepper

1. Scrub the clams and steam over a cup of boiling water until open. Remove the tough parts of the clams and coarsely chop the rest, reserving all the juice and water they steamed over and straining it through a fine sieve to remove all grit.
2. Fry the bacon a little, add the onions, and sauté a few minutes.
3. Put in a large saucepan the clam juice, bay leaf, water and all the vegetables and sautéed onions (except the potatoes) and simmer for 10 minutes.
4. Add the potatoes, salt, pepper, thyme, Worcestershire sauce and cayenne pepper and boil for a further 10 minutes.
5. Add the clams and simmer for 5 minutes or until the potatoes are done.
6. Melt the butter and add the flour and cook for 1 minute, add a little of the broth to make it smooth and then combine with the soup and cook 3 minutes and season to taste.

Serves 6-8.

Bouillabaisse (French fish soup)

haddock	2 leeks
whiting	1 bay leaf,
bass	parsley
sole	thyme
snapper	fennel
halibut	saffron
lobster	salt and pepper
12 large shrimp	white wine, dry
½ cup olive oil	2 lb (1 kg) mussels (optional)
5 garlic cloves	1 lb (500 g) scallops (optional)
2 medium onions	1 eel (optional)
4 large sized tomatoes	

1. Fillet the big fish and leave small fish whole with head and tails removed. Select six kinds of fish weighing altogether 6 lb (3 kg) when dressed.
2. The lobster needs to be cleaned and the sac removed from near the head. Cut the lobster by holding it with a towel for protection and with a large heavy sharp knife cut through the lobster near the head. Slice the tail into 5 crosswise pieces. Cut the claws from the lobster and separate the joints from the claws. Crack the flat side of each large claw. Remove the feelers and cut the body section in half lengthwise. Save the coral. Do not peel the shrimp.
3. Put the olive oil in a large heavy saucepan or kettle and add the finely chopped vegetables and herbs, first skinning the tomatoes. Cook for 5 minutes then let cool.
4. Lay the fish on top of the vegetables adding the shellfish last. If cooked lobster is used, add it to the stew the last 5 minutes. If any tender fish is cooked, add it the last 7 or 8 minutes so it won't fall apart.
5. Cover with half water and half dry white wine and let it cook no longer than 15 minutes altogether after it begins to boil.
6. Cook very gently and add salt and pepper after it has cooked 10 minutes.
7. Have buttered french bread toast in soup plates and pour the broth over it. Serve the fish on separate plates.

Serves 6-8.

Cantonese Seafood Soup

1 sole, filleted bones and
   trimmings from fish
1 onion, sliced
1 carrot, chopped
1 chicken stock cube
8 button mushrooms, halved
1 tablespoon oil
10 frozen shrimp, defrosted

1 glass dry white wine
thin spaghetti or vermicelli,
   cooked until just tender
juice of 1 lemon
salt
spinach leaves
bean sprouts

1. Place the bones and trimmings together with onion, carrot and chicken stock cube in 2 pints (1 liter) water. Bring to boil and cook for 30 minutes. Strain and put aside.
2. Cut each fillet of sole in half by slicing lengthwise. Tie each fillet loosely into a knot and poach in stock until tender.
3. Cook the mushrooms in the oil until tender, add the shrimp and stir for 2 minutes.
4. Add the dry white wine and lemon and take from the heat. Add the spinach and bring the stock again to boil. Add the rest of the ingredients except for the spaghetti.
5. When ready to serve place a coil of hot cooked spaghetti in the bottom of each bowl and ladle the soup over. Top with bean sprouts.

Serves 4.

Taramasalata

6 oz (185 g) smoked cods roe
4 slices white bread
½ onion, grated
3 cloves garlic, crushed
6 tablespoons olive oil
juice of 1 lemon
parsley

1. Soak the bread in the olive oil and blend bread and roe into a smooth paste.
2. Add onion, garlic, lemon and season with salt and pepper to taste.
3. Put into a bowl and top with parsley.

Cream may also be added to make a smooth paste or mousse-like texture.

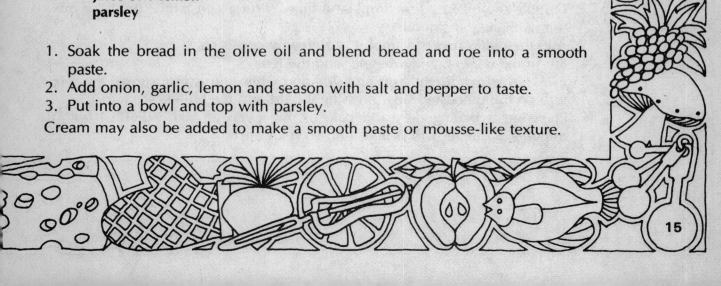

Shrimp Bisque

1 lb (500 g) cooked shrimp	6 tablespoons sherry
1 clam chowder	1 tablespoon chopped parsley
1¼ cups fresh cream, thick	1 tablespoon chopped chives
¼ teaspoon paprika	sour cream
salt and pepper	

1. Blend the shrimp and chowder in an electric blender and blend for 1 minute. (If you do not have a blender push through a sieve)
2. Add cream, sherry, parsley and bring to boil.
3. Serve immediately garnishing with a dot of sour cream and a sprinkling of chives.

Serves 6.

Anchovy Toast

2 cans flat anchovy fillets	1 teaspoon lemon juice
2 cloves garlic, crushed	10 slices french bread ½ inch
1 tablespoon olive oil	(1 cm) thick
½ cup (125 g) softened butter	1 teaspoon finely chopped
1 teaspoon wine vinegar	parsley
1 teaspoon brandy	capers
freshly ground black pepper	

1. Drain the anchovies and mash to a paste with the garlic.
2. Dribble the oil in a few drops at a time, stirring constantly, until the mixture is thick and smooth.
3. Add the butter and mix until it is a creamy consistency.
4. Stir in the wine, brandy, pepper and the lemon.
5. Brown the bread lightly on one side and while still warm, spread the mixture on the untoasted side, pressing it hard into the bread.
6. Place on a baking dish and bake in the oven at 500°F (260°C) for 10 minutes. Sprinkle with parsley and serve at once.

Smoked Salmon Rolls

   2 slices smoked salmon
      or 1 can smoked salmon
   4 oz (125 g) cream cheese
   1 tablespoon lemon juice
   1 tablespoon grated onion
   freshly ground black pepper
   chopped parsley

1. Have cheese at room temperature and mix in lemon juice, grated onion and a little pepper. Blend until very soft.
2. Spread on slices of salmon and roll up like a swiss roll and cut into 2 inch (5 cm) pieces.
3. Chill several hours before serving. Dip both ends of the rolls in chopped parsley.

Smoked Salmon Pâté

   8 oz (250 g) smoked salmon,
      chopped, minced or sliced
   2 tablespoons (40 g) butter
      or 2 tablespoons olive oil
   juice of 1 lemon
   pepper
   1 clove garlic, crushed
   chopped parsley
   3 tablespoons heavy cream

1. Blend all the ingredients except the cream together to form a smooth paste.
2. Add the cream to give a soft consistency.
3. Serve with sliced olives sprinkled on top after putting the mixture into a bowl.

17

Pancakes with Caviar

4 medium sized raw potatoes
1 onion, chopped
2 eggs
cream
salt and pepper
caviar
sour cream

1. Peel and grate the potatoes and leave in a bowl until all the liquid rises to the top. Drain well.
2. Mix the potatoes with the onion, eggs and a dash of cream and season to taste.
3. Stir the mixture well and use this mixture to make thin pancakes about 5 inches (12 cm) in diameter, in a hot buttered pan. The pancakes must be brown and crisp on both sides.
4. Pour over a spoonful of sour cream and sprinkle with caviar.

Coquilles Saint Jacques

1½ lb (750 g) scallops
1½ cups Thick Cream Sauce (see recipe)
½ cup dry white wine
1 tablespoon chopped parsley
½ teaspoon nutmeg
1 white onion, grated

4 tablespoons grated cheese
salt and pepper
8 sliced mushrooms
butter
crumbs
Parmesan cheese

1. Place scallops in a saucepan with 1 tablespoon of butter and cover and steam for 4 minutes.
2. Make a Thick Cream Sauce with the wine, parsley, nutmeg, onion and cheese added and keep hot in a double boiler. Sauté the mushrooms in a little butter.
3. Add the scallops and mushrooms to the cream sauce.
4. Place in either a shallow baking dish or individual ramekins and top with a sprinkle of crumbs and Parmesan cheese. Broil until golden brown and serve.

Serves 4-6.

Avocado and Crabmeat

1 avocado
1 can (125 g) crabmeat
3 scallions, finely chopped
1 tablespoon mayonnaise
1 teaspoon olive oil
½ teaspoon nutmeg
salt and pepper
paprika

Chop avocado and add the crabmeat, scallions, mayonnaise, oil and nutmeg.
Mix and serve in a cocktail glass over ice and sprinkle with paprika.
Serves 2.

Mushrooms with Crabmeat

10 oz (315 g) crabmeat, fresh,
   frozen or canned
2 tablespoons (40 g) butter
2 tablespoons scallions, chopped
1¼ cups Thick Cream Sauce
   (see recipe)

1 teaspoon lemon juice
nutmeg
salt and pepper
24 mushroom caps

1. Preheat the oven at 350°F (180°C).
2. Remove all the pieces of cartilage from the crabmeat and flake with a fork.
3. Melt the butter and cook the scallions until soft but not brown, stir in the crab and toss it with the scallions for 20 seconds. Transfer the mixture to a large bowl.
4. Stir the Thick Cream Sauce into the crab mixture and season to taste with the lemon juice and nutmeg.
5. Place the mushroom caps on a greased baking sheet and sprinkle them with salt, spoon in the crab filling and bake in the top part of the oven for 15 minutes or until mushrooms are tender.

Serves 4.

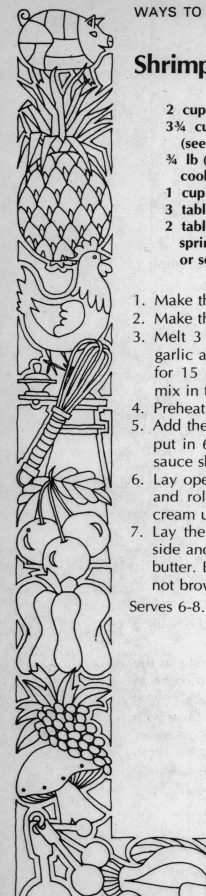

Shrimp Pancakes

2 cups pancake mix
3¾ cups (900 ml) Thick Cream Sauce
  (see recipe)
¾ lb (375 g) chopped
  cooked shrimp
1 cup chopped mushrooms
3 tablespoons (60 g) butter
2 tablespoons chopped
  spring onions
  or scallions

1 teaspoon chopped parsley
1 teaspoon cut chives
salt and pepper
lemon juice
4 oz (125 g) Gruyere cheese
3 tablespoons (60 g) butter

1. Make the pancakes, about 16, and put aside.
2. Make the Thick Cream Sauce following the recipe. Put aside.
3. Melt 3 tablespoons butter and stir in the spring onions or scallions and garlic and cook until soft, do not brown. Stir in the mushrooms and cook for 15 minutes until all the moisture has evaporated. Put in a bowl and mix in the parsley and chives. Season to taste.
4. Preheat the oven at 375°F (190°C).
5. Add the chopped cooked shrimp to the mushroom and onion mixture and put in 6 tablespoons of the Thick Cream Sauce or more if necessary, the sauce should be thick enough to hold its shape.
6. Lay open the pancakes and place a large tablespoon full on the pancake and roll up. Do not tuck in the ends. Thin the rest of the sauce with cream until it flows heavily off a spoon.
7. Lay the pancakes in a greased oven proof dish, arranging them side by side and pour the sauce over them and sprinkle with cheese and dot with butter. Bake in the upper part of the oven for 20 minutes. If the top is still not brown pop under a broiler.

Serves 6-8.

Oysters Au Gratin

oysters on the half shell
lemon juice
fine crumbs
grated parmesan cheese

1. Squeeze 3 or 4 drops of lemon on each oyster and cover lightly with a mixture of fine crumbs and parmesan cheese.
2. Place under a broiler and cook until the cheese and crumbs become brown.

Fried Oysters

6 oysters per person
salt and pepper
fine cracker crumbs
beaten egg
hot oil or butter and lard
lemon juice and chopped parsley

1. Drain the oysters for an hour. Never wash. Dry and roll lightly in seasoned bread or cracker crumbs.
2. Dip them in the beaten egg and again roll them in the crumbs.
3. Melt enough oil or butter and lard to make it ½ inch (1 cm) deep in the frying pan and make it quite hot.
4. Fry the oysters a light golden brown on each side and serve immediately with parsley and lemon juice.

These are also delicious served with Tartare Sauce (see recipe).

Oyster Bisque

1½ cups chopped celery	30 small oysters
½ cup chopped onion	salt
1 chopped green pepper	pepper
3 tablespoons (60 g) butter	1 teaspoon paprika
1 cup oyster liquor	pinch thyme
5 cups (1200 ml) fish stock	dash nutmeg
or milk	dash cayenne

1. Put celery, onion and green pepper into a blender and purée.
2. Sauté in butter for 4 or 5 minutes. Add the strained oyster liquor and the milk or fish stock to the vegetables and cook for a further 10 minutes. Blend in the blender again. Season to taste, heat up and add the oysters. A dash of brandy may be added if desired.

Oysters Rockefeller

oysters on half a shell
6 green onions
handful each of fresh spinach and
    parsley
celery leaves (tender)
tarragon
⅓ cup (90 g) butter
salt and freshly ground black pepper
Tabasco sauce
bread crumbs

1. Blanch the greens in a little salt water. Strain and push through a sieve. Mix the puree with the softened butter and season with salt, pepper and a dash of Tabasco sauce.
2. Put a spoonful on each oyster and a very slight layer of breadcrumbs.
3. Place under a broiler for about 5 minutes. When oysters begin to curl remove and serve immediately.

Salads and Cold Dishes

Salmon Ring

1 tablespoon gelatin
2 tablespoons cold water
¾ cup (187 ml) hot water
½ cup (125 ml) white wine
1 teaspoon sugar
2 tablespoons lemon juice
sliced hard-boiled eggs
avocado
cucumber
olives

2 cups flaked canned
   salmon or tuna
2 tablespoons gelatin
½ cup mayonnaise
¼ cup cream
½ cup chopped tender celery
sliced tomatoes, avocado,
   greens and mayonnaise

1. Make the aspic by soaking the gelatin in the cold water a few minutes and dissolving it in the hot water.
2. When cool add the wine, sugar and lemon juice. Instead of wine a weak vinegar and more sugar may be used.
3. Pour half of the aspic into a greased mold and arrange some sliced egg, avocado, cucumber and olives in the bottom and let it set. Then add the rest of the aspic and more of the garnishes.
4. Soak 2 teaspoons gelatin in the cold water and then dissolve it *over* the hot water and add it to the cream and mayonnaise.
5. Mix in the fish lightly and add more seasoning if required.
6. Add this to the hardened aspic and chill until set.
7. Unmold the garnish with greens, sliced vegetables and mayonnaise.

Serves 6-8.

Salmon Rice Salad

1½ cups cooked rice
¼ cup french dressing
¾ cup mayonnaise
½ teaspoon salt
¼ teaspoon pepper
1 tablespoon finely
   chopped onion
1 teaspoon horseradish sauce

½ teaspoon celery salt
   or seed
½ cup chopped celery
1 chopped hard-boiled egg
½ cup sliced cucumber, peeled
1 cup flaked cooked salmon
   or tuna

1. While rice is hot add the french dressing.
2. Cool to room temperature before adding rest of ingredients. Mix lightly.
3. Chill at least 1 hour before serving.

Serves 6-8.

Tuna Salad Spanish Style

6 oz (185 g) tuna
1 tablespoon olive oil
2 tablespoons dry sherry
1 medium onion, sliced
½ green pepper, chopped
2 tablespoons parsley, chopped

Drain the tuna, add olive oil and remaining ingredients and toss. Chill for at least 2 hours and serve.

Serves 2.

Bean and Tuna Salad

1 can (large) tuna	chopped parsley
1 can of lima (or butter) beans	1 clove garlic chopped
olive oil	salt
vinegar	pepper
1 tablespoon chopped spring onions	mayonnaise

1. Drain the cans of tuna and beans and mix together in a large bowl.
2. Add the oil and vinegar, to taste. The proportion of oil to vinegar should be 3:1.
3. Mix in the spring onions, chopped parsley, garlic, salt and pepper to taste.
4. Add enough mayonnaise to cover the mixture.

A hard-boiled egg or two can be sliced and added with a sprinkle of caviar for variety.

Serves 6.

Cold Mackerel Spanish Style

6 fresh mackerel	8 tablespoons vinegar
3 medium tomatoes	8 tablespoons olive oil
1 green pepper	salt and pepper
3 scallions, finely chopped	thyme, tarragon, crushed bay leaf
1 large lemon	1 lemon sliced
¾ cup dry white wine	

1. Place the cleaned fish in a large pan.
2. Peel the tomatoes and chop them into medium sized chunks. Seed and chop the pepper and mix finely chopped scallions and tomatoes in a saucepan.
3. Slice the lemon into thin slices and add to the vegetable mixture.
4. Add the dry white wine, vinegar and olive oil. Season with salt and pepper and add the other seasonings. Cook for 15 minutes and pour the hot mixture over the mackerel.
5. Put the pan containing fish over a medium heat and bring to the boil. Lower the heat and cook fish for 10 to 15 minutes. Cool then chill at least 2 hours, garnish with sliced lemon.

Serves 6.

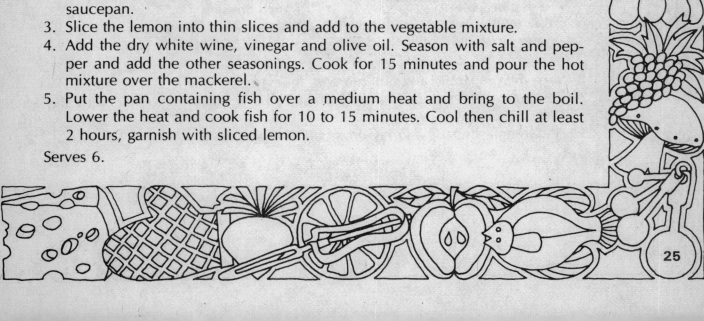

Whiting in Aspic

1½ lb (750 g) whiting fillets	6 peppercorns
fish and fish trimmings	salt
for stock	3 egg whites
2½ cups (600 ml) water	stuffed olives
1½ cups dry white wine	2 hard-boiled eggs, sliced
1 bay leaf	water, wine, onion, herbs for
1 carrot, sliced	poaching the fish
1 onion, sliced	

1. Simmer all the ingredients together except the egg whites and the whiting, for 20 minutes, put in the egg whites and stir quickly for 1 minute. Strain and set aside to cool.
2. When cool, pour ½ inch (1 cm) of the stock into a shallow ovenproof or pyrex dish and place in the refrigerator and set. Put aside remaining stock.
3. Gently poach the fillets in a mixture of water, white wine and a peeled onion, season to taste. Let the fish cool and carefully remove its skin.
4. Place the olives and hard-boiled eggs decoratively over the set aspic and arrange the fillets over them. Pour over the rest of the unset stock or aspic and put in refrigerator to set. At least 3 hours.
5. Unmold on a serving dish and serve with Tartare Sauce, Hollandaise Sauce, Mayonnaise, Egg Sauce or any other sauces suggested for cold fish (see recipes).

Sole or other white fish can be used for this dish and must be skinned.

Serves 6.

Pineapple and Shrimp Salad

fresh pineapple	french dressing
1 lb (500 g) peeled sliced shrimp	watercress or crisp greens
water chestnuts (optional)	

1. Slice the pineapple and cut into very thin slices.
2. Peel and slice the chestnuts and mix all ingredients together with the sliced shrimp.
3. Add french dressing and lay on a bed of crisp greens.

Serves 4.

Crab Mousse

2 cups of fresh flaked crabmeat	¼ cup mayonnaise
1 tablespoon gelatin	¾ cup cream, heavy
3 tablespoons cold water	salt and pepper
1 tablespoon chopped parsley	sliced hard-boiled eggs
1 tablespoon chopped chives or green onions	tomatoes
	cucumber
1 tablespoon ketchup	shrimp
2 tablespoons lemon juice	green olives

1. Bone the crabmeat. Soak the gelatin in the cold water and dissolve over hot water.
2. Add the gelatin to the mayonnaise and mix with all the other ingredients.
3. Fold in the crabmeat and thick whipped cream, pour into a greased mold and chill.
4. Unmold on a large platter and garnish with sliced egg, tomatoes, cucumber, shrimp and olives.

Serve with mayonnaise.

Serves 4-6.

Shrimp Mousse

1 lb (500 g) cooked fresh shrimp	1 cup diced celery
8 oz (250 g) cream cheese	1 medium onion, grated
1 can (about 375 ml) tomato purée	salt and pepper
1½ tablespoons gelatin	1 cup mayonnaise
½ cup (125 ml) cold water	

1. Peel the shrimp. Cut lengthwise and remove the black vein.
2. Melt the cream cheese in the tomato purée, and when smooth dissolve the gelatin (which has been soaked in the cold water for 3 minutes) in the hot mixture.
3. Use the tender stalks of the celery and cut them very fine. When the purée mixture is cool combine all the ingredients and pour them into a greased mold or ring.
4. When ready to serve unmold and fill or garnish with tomato or avocado slices or some lettuce.

This will serve 10 or 12. Half the recipe will serve 6 and be used as an appetizer or as a salad.

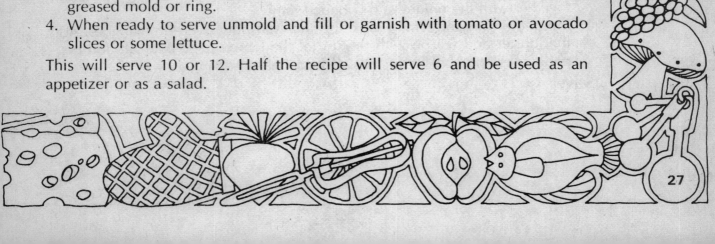

Southern Style Crab

1¼ cups (300 ml) mayonnaise
2 tablespoons tomato sauce
Worcestershire sauce
Tabasco sauce
3 tablespoons olive oil
1 tablespoon wine vinegar
2 tablespoons grated onion
2 tablespoons chopped parsley
1 tablespoon lemon rind, grated
1 tablespoon lemon juice

6 tablespoons sour cream
salt, freshly ground black
   pepper
2 tablespoons chopped olives
1 lb (500 g) cooked crabmeat,
   flaked
6 large tomatoes
lettuce and sliced hard-
   boiled eggs

1. Mix together the mayonnaise, tomato sauce, Worcestershire and Tabasco sauce, oil, vinegar, onion, parsley, lemon juice, lemon rind and whipped sour cream. Season to taste. Stir in the chopped olives and chill for at least 2 hours.
2. Just before serving add flaked crabmeat and slice the tomatoes in half, place on salad plates and pile the crab salad on the tomatoes. Garnish with lettuce and sliced hard-boiled eggs.

This sauce is delicious for all seafood cocktails.

Serves 4-6.

Mango and Lobster Salad

1 lobster
2 large mangoes
1 tablespoon spring onions,
   chopped
1 cup cream

2 tablespoons lemon juice
1 tablespoon freshly
   chopped mint
salt
freshly ground black pepper

1. Prepare lobster by removing vein and sac from near the head. Remove from shell and slice into 3 inches (8 cm) pieces. Sprinkle with 1 tablespoon of the lemon and juice and set aside.
2. Peel and slice and remove the stone from the mangoes. Place in a bowl together with the onions and chopped mint.
3. Mix the cream and lemon juice together and pour over the mangoes. Add the lobster and season with the rest of the lemon juice and salt and pepper. Cover and chill for at least 1 hour, before serving.

Serves 4-6.

Shrimp Remoulade

2 lbs (1 kg) shrimp
1 cup Oil Mayonnaise (see recipe)
2 tablespoons chopped sweet pickle
2 teaspoons German mustard
2 tablespoons chopped parsley
2 tablespoons capers
1 to 4 tablespoons salad
  dressing

1. Shell the shrimp and remove veins and mix together with all the other ingredients making sure the dressing added to the sauce gives a thick cream consistency.
2. Chill in refrigerator for at least 1 hour before serving.

Serve on shredded lettuce.

Serves 8 or 10.

Shrimp Southern Style

1 cup (250 ml) dry white wine
3 cups shrimp
1 cup mayonnaise
1 tablespoon prepared mustard
1 tablespoon lemon juice
1 tablespoon finely chopped
  parsley
1 tablespoon capers, chopped

1 clove garlic, crushed
1 teaspoon grated onion
salt and pepper
2 cups celery, chopped
1 cup cucumber, peeled,
  seeded and chopped
lettuce leaves
paprika

1. Pour wine over shrimp (chop shrimp if large) cover and chill for at least 2 hours, turning occasionally.
2. Mix mayonnaise, mustard, lemon juice, parsley, capers, garlic and onion, season with salt and pepper to taste.
3. Drain the shrimp and add them with the celery and cucumber to the mayonnaise mixture. Serve on lettuce leaves and sprinkle with paprika.

Serves 6-8.

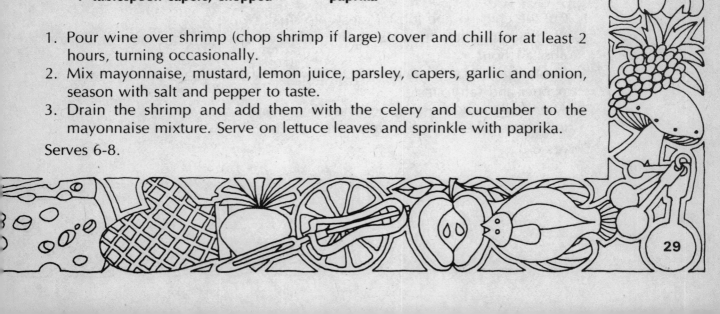

Lobster and Potato Salad

½ cup olive oil	3 tablespoons heavy cream
2 tablespoons wine vinegar	½ cup onion, grated
salt and pepper	2 tablespoons chopped parsley
3 cups boiled sliced potatoes	1 teaspoon lemon juice
½ cup peeled and diced cucumber	rind from 1 lemon
2 1½ lb (750 g) lobsters,	nutmeg
cooked and chilled	parsley or fresh basil
¾ cup mayonnaise	tomato slices

1. In a large mixing bowl stir oil with a fork and add vinegar gradually until it is all absorbed. Add salt, pepper, potatoes and cucumbers. Toss gently so as not to break the potatoes and let stand for 2 hours. Drain and add 1 inch (2 cm) cubes of lobster meat, mayonnaise, cream, onions, parsley and lemon juice and lemon rind. Mix well and chill.
2. When ready to serve add parsley or basil and tomato slices to garnish.

Serves 4-6.

Lobster and Chicken Salad

1 lb (500 g) chicken breasts, cooked	cayenne pepper
1 lb (500 g) cooked lobster meat	1 tablespoon chopped chives
french dressing	½ cup cream, whipped
3 hard-boiled eggs	2 cups shredded lettuce or cabbage
1 cup celery, chopped	parsley, chopped
1 cup Oil Mayonnaise (see recipe)	

1. Cut the chicken and lobster meat into small strips.
2. Marinate in a little french dressing with chopped egg whites and celery for about 1 hour.
3. Mash egg yolks and blend with Oil Mayonnaise, chives and parsley, cayenne pepper and salt to taste.
4. After chilling the dressing, add the chicken and lobster and serve on a bed of lettuce or cabbage and sprinkle with parsley.

Serves 6-8.

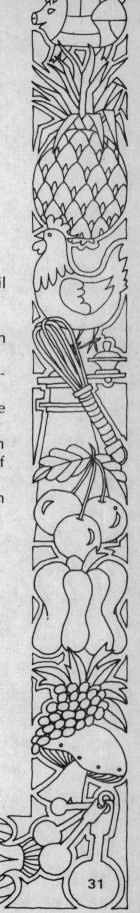

Fish and Lobster Mousse (Cold)

1½ lbs (750 g) salmon (canned
   salmon or tuna)
½ cup cream
½ cup Oil Mayonnaise
   (see recipe)
1 tablespoon gelatin
2 tablespoons cold water
salt and pepper
1½ cups (375 ml) chicken broth

2 teaspoons gelatin
2 tablespoons cold water
1 lb (500 g) fresh cooked
   lobster meat or shrimp
Oil Mayonnaise, capers,
   sour cream
curry powder
   or dash of mustard

1. Steam the fish until tender, remove the skin and bone it.
2. Push the fish through a sieve and mash to a paste with the cream and Oil Mayonnaise.
3. Add salt and pepper to taste.
4. Soak the 1 tablespoon gelatin in the cold water for a few minutes then dissolve over hot water and add to the fish paste.
5. Make a clear aspic by heating the chicken broth and dissolving 2 teaspoons gelatin which has been soaked in the cold water.
6. Cut the lobster into 1 inch (2½ cm) sized pieces or cut shrimp the same size.
7. Cool the aspic and in a greased mold, alternate the layers of the gelatin fish paste with the chicken aspic. Put the lobster or shrimp in the layers of the chicken aspic, letting each layer set before adding the other.
8. Chill with Oil Mayonnaise thinned with a little sour cream seasoned with the capers and a dash of curry powder or mustard.

Serves 4-6.

Green Lobster Salad

1 lobster, cooked
1 cucumber, peeled, seeded and diced
2 hard-boiled eggs, diced
3 large ripe avocado pears
juice of 3 lemons
finely chopped chives
parsley, finely chopped

Green Sauce:
⅔ cup Oil Mayonnaise (see recipe)
4 tablespoons puréed spinach
nutmeg
salt and pepper
lemon juice

1. Cut up the lobster into 1 inch (2 ½ cm) cubes, prepare the cucumber and hard-boiled eggs. Slice the avocado pears in half, remove the seeds and take out the flesh with a sharp knife in pieces about ½ inch (1 cm) square. Try not to pierce the skin with the knife. Remove the flesh and marinate in lemon juice and brush the insides of the avocado shells with lemon juice. Put aside.
2. Make the green sauce by mixing Oil Mayonnaise with the puréed spinach and season to taste with salt, pepper and a little lemon juice.
3. Combine the diced avocado, cucumber, lobster and eggs in a large bowl and add the green sauce tossing carefully. Fill the avocado shells with mixture and chill for at least 1 hour.

Serve with a sprinkle of chopped chives and parsley.

Serves 4-6.

Sauces and Stuffings

Anchovy Sauce

   3 tablespoons anchovy paste
      or 3 anchovy fillets
   ½ cup Oil Mayonnaise
      (see recipe) or sour cream

Blend the paste with the Oil Mayonnaise or sour cream.

Veloute Sauce

   2 tablespoons (40 g) butter
   2 tablespoons flour
   ½ cup cream
   ½ cup fish stock

1. Melt the butter and add the flour, until smooth.
2. Slowly stir in the cream and very strong fish stock.
3. Cook for 5 minutes.

This is a very basic fish sauce.

Tomato Sour Cream Sauce

1 cup tomato sauce
⅔ cup sour cream
1 tablespoon chilli powder
   or 1 teaspoon fennel,
   or 1 teaspoon curry powder
   or mustard
salt and pepper

Mix and heat the tomato sauce with sour cream and add your chosen seasoning.

Thick Cream Sauce

2 tablespoons (40 g) butter
4 tablespoons flour
1 cup (250 ml) cream
salt and pepper

Melt the butter in a saucepan and mix in the flour until a smooth paste. Cook over low heat for 2 minutes. Take off from heat and gradually add the cream until smooth. Heat slowly and cook until very thick and smooth.

Tomato and Cheese Sauce

1 onion, minced
½ green pepper, minced
3 tablespoons (60 g) butter
   or olive oil
salt and pepper

1⅓ cups (350 ml) canned
   tomato purée
½ teaspoon fennel
½ cup (60 g) grated sharp
   cheese

1. Sauté the onion and green pepper in butter or oil for 3 minutes.
2. Add the salt, pepper and puree and simmer again for 10 minutes.
3. Add fennel and cheese and stir until the cheese is melted. Take off the heat immediately.

This is an excellent sauce for serving with fish or when mixed with sour cream poured over a large fish and baked.

Ravigote Sauce for Mussels or Clams

2 tablespoons (40 g) butter
1 tablespoon flour
½ can beef consomme
2 egg yolks beaten
salt and pepper
½ teaspoon mustard
2 tablespoons lemon juice
6 scallions or chopped
green onions

1. Melt the butter and blend in the flour and slowly add the consomme.
2. Cook until it thickens stirring constantly.
3. Keep hot in the top of the double boiler until ready to serve. Then add beaten egg yolks quickly and add the chopped scallions or onions.

Tartare Sauce

1 cup Oil Mayonnaise
(see recipe)
1 tablespoon ground onion
1 tablespoon ground parsley
1 tablespoon chopped chives
1 tablespoon chopped pickles
1 tablespoon chopped green
olives
1 tablespoon whole capers
dash paprika

Mix all ingredients with the Oil Mayonnaise.
This sauce is for any type of fish but is best served with fried seafood such as fried oysters, scallops etc.

Shrimp Sauce

1 lb (500 g) unshelled shrimp	2 tablespoons (40 g) butter
⅔ cup (100 ml) water	3 tablespoons flour
salt and pepper	¼ teaspoon nutmeg
1 bay leaf	1 cup cream
1 tablespoon grated onion	2 egg yolks
2 tablespoons lemon juice	3 tablespoons sherry

1. Wash but do not shell the shrimp; these give flavor to the stock.
2. Bring the shrimp slowly to a simmer in the water, salt, pepper, bay leaf, onion and lemon juice. Let simmer for 5 minutes. Cool.
3. Peel the shrimp and use the stock in making the sauce.
4. Melt the butter, blend in the flour and when smooth add the shrimp stock. When it thickens a little, add the cream, nutmeg and season again if necessary.
5. When ready to serve, beat in the egg yolks and add the shrimp which have been cut into small pieces. Add the sherry.

This sauce is for serving with baked fish, on toast or in patty shells.

Mornay Sauce

1 cup (250 ml) rich cream sauce	Rich Cream Sauce:
2 tablespoons grated Parmesan cheese	1 tablespoon (20 g) butter
	1 tablespoon flour
	½ teaspoon salt
2 tablespoons grated Swiss cheese or Cheddar	1 cup (250 ml) cream
	½ teaspoon pepper
¼ cup white wine	1 egg yolk

1. Make the rich cream sauce by melting the butter in a saucepan adding the flour and stir until smooth. Add the salt and milk very slowly stirring continuously so it won't be lumpy. Add the pepper and cook for 5 minutes over low heat. When finished stir in beaten egg yolk.
2. Add cheese and wine just before serving.

This sauce is appropriate for baked fish.

Lobster Sauce

1 lb (500 g) fresh lobster meat	3 egg yolks, beaten
brandy or sherry	salt and pepper
1½ tablespoons flour	½ teaspoon nutmeg
4 tablespoons (80 g) butter	3 tablespoons brandy or sherry
1½ cups cream	

1. Cut the lobster in good sized pieces and mix it with 2 tablespoons of the butter, melted, and a sprinkle of brandy or sherry and let stand for 10 minutes.
2. Melt the rest of the butter in the top part of a double boiler, blend in the flour and add the cream.
3. Cook for 5 minutes and slowly pour in the beaten egg yolks.
4. Add the seasonings and the lobster. When hot, add the 3 tablespoons brandy or sherry.

This sauce is delicious served with noodles, rice, or to pour over boiled fish.

Lemon Butter Sauce

½ cup (125 g) melted butter
salt
freshly ground black pepper
juice of 2 lemons
2 tablespoons fine dry breadcrumbs

Mix all ingredients together.
This is nice served with shrimp, lobster and broiled fish.

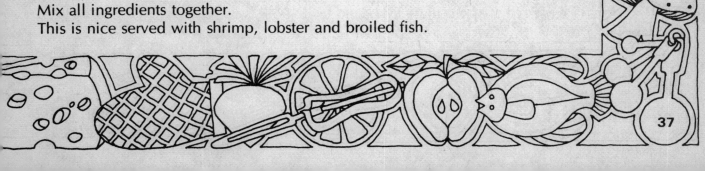

37

Egg Sauce

2 hard-boiled eggs
½ teaspoon Worcestershire sauce
1 teaspoon lemon rind
4 tablespoons lemon juice
dash nutmeg
1 egg yolk
1 tablespoon fresh onion juice

Cream Sauce:
2 tablespooons (40 g) butter
1 tablespoon flour
½ cup (125 ml) milk
½ cup cream
salt and pepper
½ teaspoon paprika

1. Make a cream sauce by melting the butter and adding the flour and then the milk and cream slowly, cook until it thickens and season with salt and pepper and paprika.
2. Return to heat and add the Worcestershire sauce, lemon rind, lemon juice, nutmeg and onion juice and hard-boiled eggs and cook for 2 minutes.
3. Add the beaten egg yolks just before serving.

Creole Sauce

4 tablespoons (80 g) butter
2 onions, chopped
4 stalks celery, chopped
¾ cup sliced mushrooms
1 teaspoon salt
1 tablespoon flour
1 teaspoon pepper

2 tablespoons chilli powder
1 green pepper, chopped
2 teaspoons brown sugar
1 tablespoon vinegar
2 cups tomatoes, mashed
½ teaspoon basil
12 green olives, sliced

1. Sauté celery and onions in butter for 4 minutes and add the mushrooms and cook another 2 minutes.
2. Stir in the flour and add all the other ingredients and simmer 20 minutes.

Cream and Onion Sauce

1 lb (500 g) white onions,
 sliced
½ cup (125 g) butter
1 cup Rich, Thick Cream
 Sauce
dash nutmeg or mace
¼ cup (60 ml) cream

Rich, Thick Cream Sauce:
2 tablespoons (40 g) butter
4 tablespoons flour
1 cup cream
salt and pepper

1. Make the Rich Thick Cream Sauce by melting the butter in a saucepan and mixing in the flour and gradually adding the cream to make a smooth paste. Heat slowly and cook until very thick. Put aside.
2. Cook the onions in the butter and when they are soft mash through a sieve. Add these to the thick cream sauce.
3. Season and serve over boiled or broiled fish.

Cocktail Sauce

½ cup (125 ml) cream
1½ tablespoons lemon juice
2 tablespoons ground onion
 or chopped chives
½ cup tomato sauce
dash Tabasco sauce
dash Worcestershire sauce

Mix all the ingredients together and season with salt and pepper to taste.

Black Butter Sauce

5 tablespoons (100 g) butter
2 tablespoons fresh onion
  juice
2 tablespoons lemon juice
2 tablespoons capers
salt and pepper

1. Brown the butter in a saucepan without burning it.
2. Add other ingredients.

This sauce is suitable for broiled or fried fish.

Green Mayonnaise

1¼ cups (300 ml) Oil Mayonnaise (see recipe)
2 tablespoons tarragon
2 tablespoons fresh parsley, chopped
2 tablespoons fresh chives,
  chopped
2 tablespoons grated onion
1 teaspoon fennel (optional)
2 tablespoons lemon juice

1. Mix all the ingredients together and add the fennel if necessary.
2. Add salt and freshly ground black pepper.

This is served with cold boiled fish or fish salads.

Mayonnaise Cream Sauce for Lobster

1 cup Oil Mayonnaise
(see recipe)
¼ cup (60 ml) dry
white wine

½ cup heavy cream or sour cream
parsley
dash tarragon

Mix all the ingredients together.
This sauce can be served hot or cold. If the lobster is hot, a little melted butter may be added to the lobster.

Oil Mayonnaise

2 egg yolks
⅛ teaspoon sugar
1 teaspoon salt
½ teaspoon vinegar
1 cup (250 ml) olive oil
lemon juice or vinegar
pepper
paprika

1. Make sure all the ingredients are at room temperature.
2. Beat egg yolks with sugar, salt, vinegar and mustard, until thick.
3. Add the oil drop by drop at first and when it begins to thicken add it a little faster. Add seasonings to taste.

This can be made with a rotary beater, hand beater or in the electric blender. The mayonnaise can be thinned with lemon juice or vinegar.

Parmesan and Mayonnaise Sauce for Fish

½ cup Oil Mayonnaise
   (see recipe)
⅓ cup Parmesan cheese
2 teaspoons basil
2 teaspoons German mustard
2 teaspoons Angostura bitters

Mix all the ingredients together.
This is nice served warm or cold.

Sour Cream Mayonnaise

½ cup Oil Mayonnaise
   (see recipe)
½ cup sour cream
1 tablespoon lemon juice
1 teaspoon curry powder
1 tablespoon fresh onion juice

Mix all ingredients together.

Mushroom and Tomato Stuffing

1 cup (125 g) mushrooms, chopped
3 large tomatoes, skinned and chopped
1 tablespoon parsley
3 tablespoons (60 g) melted butter
½ cup breadcrumbs
salt and pepper

Mix all the ingredients together and season to taste.
This is suitable for all kinds of fish.

Celery and Apple Stuffing

4 sticks celery, chopped
2 peeled apples, chopped
1 tablespoon onion, grated
salt and pepper
1 tablespoon raisins
½ teaspoon honey
½ cup breadcrumbs
3 tablespoons (60 g) butter, melted

Mix all the ingredients thoroughly together.

This stuffing is suitable for large fish as it is hard to handle due to the lumpy consistency. It is nice to use cooked on its own and served with the fish. It is suitable for strong tasting fish e.g. mackerel.

Asparagus and Onion Stuffing

1 small can of cooked asparagus
   or 1 bunch, cooked
⅔ cup (60 g) breadcrumbs
3 tablespoons (60 g) butter
1 onion, grated

1. Chop the stalk ends from a small can of asparagus or a bunch of asparagus. Put aside the tips for garnishing.
2. Mix the stalk ends of asparagus, breadcrumbs, melted butter and onion together. This should be suitable for most fish especially fish with a delicate flavor.

Fish

Sole Scandinavian

1 lb (500 g) fillets of sole
flour
salt and pepper
2 tablespoons lemon juice
¼ cup cream
½ teaspoon fresh parsley
½ teaspoon nutmeg
½ cup chopped almond
    flakes
paprika

1. Dip the sole into seasoned flour.
2. Place in a fry pan and cook in butter for 3 minutes each side.
3. Meanwhile mix lemon juice, cream, parsley and nutmeg together and add salt and pepper to taste, heat in pan for 5 minutes.
4. When sole is cooked transfer to a large platter and spread with the cream sauce and sprinkle with paprika and parsley.

Serves 4.

Whiting in a Tomato and Wine Sauce

2 tablespoons (40 g) butter
1 onion, grated
2 tomatoes, peeled and sliced
lemon
salt and pepper
4 whiting fillets

1 cup (250 ml) dry white wine
parsley
butter
flour
cream

1. Place the onion, tomatoes and slices of 1 lemon in a greased, ovenproof dish and season with salt and pepper.
2. Place the fillets on top and pour on the wine. Sprinkle with parsley and bake in a hot oven for 10 minutes.
3. Place the fish on a hot serving dish put aside and keep warm. Drain the liquid from the baked fish into a saucepan and bring to the boil, add 1 tablespoon of butter and 1 tablespoon of flour mixed together. Stir consistently and cook very slowly for 7 minutes. Add a little cream and pour the sauce over the fish and garnish with some chopped parsley.

Serves 4.

Baked Fillets of Sole with Shellfish

fillets of sole
salt and pepper
8 raw peeled shrimp
8 mussels
3 tablespoons (60 g) melted butter

½ cup sliced mushroom, sauteed
2 tablespoons lemon juice
¼ cup (63 ml) dry white wine
2 beaten egg yolks
½ cup scalded cream

1. Lay the fish in a baking dish and sprinkle salt and pepper over them.
2. Cover the fish with shrimp, mussels, sauteed mushrooms and place some around the fish, add the melted butter, lemon juice and wine and bake until done, 15 to 20 minutes.
3. Scald the cream and add to the beaten egg yolks and pour over the fish. If sauce is still not thickened, a little cornstarch may be used.
4. Sprinkle with Parmesan and a little chopped parsley.

Serves 4-6.

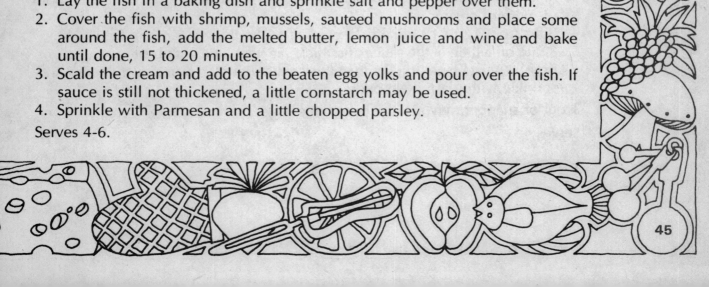

Sole and Lemon

4 small to medium sized sole
  or other white fish
salt and pepper
3 tablespoons (60 g) butter
2 small onions
2 lemons
parsley

1. Season the fish lightly and place each fish if whole or 2 fillets onto a piece of greased aluminum foil.
2. Peel the onions and slice thinly and place over the fish together with sliced lemons. Top with the remaining butter and wrap the foil firmly around the fish.
3. Place on a baking tray and bake in moderate oven for about 35 minutes.
4. When ready to serve open foil and sprinkle with parsley.

Serves 4.

Baked Sole with Almonds

3 lb (1½ kg) fillets of sole   olive oil
3 tablespoons (60 g) butter   cream
⅓ cup chopped onion   ¼ cup (63 ml) white wine
½ cup sliced mushroom   flour or egg yolk
2 tablespoons chopped parsley   ½ cup browned sliced almonds
salt and pepper

1. Rub the fillets with olive oil and a little salt and pepper.
2. Sauté the vegetables 2 or 3 minutes in the butter and lay them on the bottom of a baking dish.
3. Place fillets on the vegetables and baste with the white wine and a tablespoon or more of cream.
4. Bake from 12 to 18 minutes according to the thickness of the fish.
5. Strain off a little of the sauce and thicken a very little with beaten egg yolk or flour. It must be not thicker than this cream. Pour the sauce over the fish and sprinkle with toasted almonds.

Trout or snapper may also be baked this way.

Serves 4.

Sole French Style

- 4 fillets of sole
- 4 tablespoons (80 g) butter
- salt and pepper
- 3 tablespoons grated onion
- ½ lb (500 g) sliced mushrooms
- 4 tablespoons Burgundy style
  red wine

1. Wash the fish, wipe dry and lay them on a well buttered baking dish. Sprinkle salt and pepper on both sides of fish and add grated onion, sliced mushrooms and wine, pouring the ingredients over the fish.
2. Bake 15 minutes in a hot oven 400°F (200°C).

Serves 4.

The sauce may be thickened with a little cornstarch.

Sole with Grapes

- 4 large or 8 smaller fillets
  of sole, whiting or any other
  white fish
- salt and pepper
- thyme
- 2 tablespoons (40 g) butter
- 2 cups (500 ml) white wine
- 1 tablespoon flour
- ¼ pint (150 ml) milk
- 3 tablespoons cream
- 1 cup green seeded grapes
- 1 lemon

1. Roll or fold the fillets of fish, put into a greased baking dish and season with salt and pepper and a sprinkle of thyme.
2. Pour over half the butter and the wine. Add the grapes, cover and cook in a moderate oven 350°F (180°C) for about 20 minutes.
3. Meanwhile heat the remainder of the butter in a saucepan, stir in the flour and continue stirring over a low heat for 3 minutes.
4. Add the milk and bring to the boil and stir until the sauce thickens.
5. Lift the fish onto a hot plate and strain the remaining liquid from the fish into the sauce. Stir in the cream and heat again without boiling. Pour over the baked fish.
6. Serve and garnish with sliced lemon and some grapes (optional).

Serves 4.

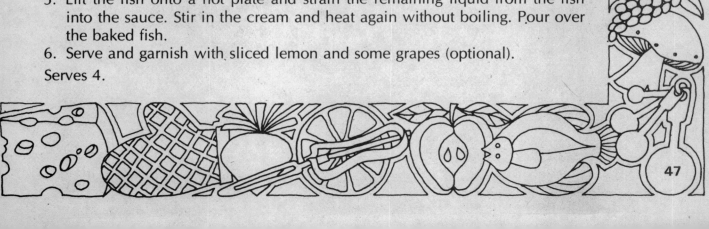

Sole Normandie

4 fillets of sole	125 g (4 0z) mushrooms, sliced
1 lb (500 g) mussels	2 tablespoons flour
4 scallions, chopped	½ cup (125 ml) wine
or 1 white onion, chopped	⅓ cup cream
butter	2 egg yolks
¼ cup (63 ml) water	parsley
bay leaf	
½ teaspoon thyme	

1. Scrub the mussels.
2. Bring the water, shallots or onion, bay leaf and thyme to boil for 4 minutes, add half the wine and steam the mussels over this until they open.
3. Remove the mussels from the shells and set aside.
4. Strain the broth through a fine sieve.
5. Place the fillets of fish in a long baking dish, which can be taken to the table, and add the broth to them.
6. Bake in a 375°F (190°C) oven for 10 minutes or until they are done. Do not overcook.
7. Sauté the sliced mushrooms in a little butter. Melt two tablespoons (40 g) butter in a saucepan, add two tablespoons flour and when smooth, slowly add the broth from the fish.
8. Drain the fish well to avoid thinning the sauce. Cook for 3 minutes then add the mushrooms, mussels, rest of the wine and scalded cream which has been poured over the beaten egg yolks. Taste and season. Do not boil the sauce. When hot pour over the fish and serve.

Serves 4.

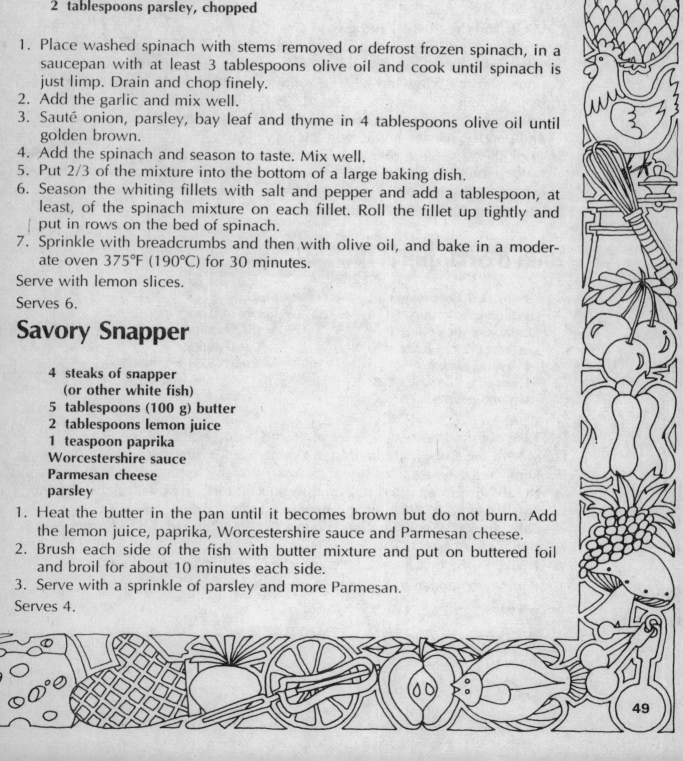

Stuffed Whiting

6 small whitings, filleted
3 lbs (1½ kg) fresh spinach
   or 1 lb (500 g) frozen spinach
7 tablespoons olive oil
2 cloves garlic, crushed
1 large onion, chopped
2 tablespoons parsley, chopped

1 bay leaf, crumbled
thyme
salt and pepper
fresh breadcrumbs
lemon slices

1. Place washed spinach with stems removed or defrost frozen spinach, in a saucepan with at least 3 tablespoons olive oil and cook until spinach is just limp. Drain and chop finely.
2. Add the garlic and mix well.
3. Sauté onion, parsley, bay leaf and thyme in 4 tablespoons olive oil until golden brown.
4. Add the spinach and season to taste. Mix well.
5. Put 2/3 of the mixture into the bottom of a large baking dish.
6. Season the whiting fillets with salt and pepper and add a tablespoon, at least, of the spinach mixture on each fillet. Roll the fillet up tightly and put in rows on the bed of spinach.
7. Sprinkle with breadcrumbs and then with olive oil, and bake in a moderate oven 375°F (190°C) for 30 minutes.

Serve with lemon slices.

Serves 6.

Savory Snapper

4 steaks of snapper
   (or other white fish)
5 tablespoons (100 g) butter
2 tablespoons lemon juice
1 teaspoon paprika
Worcestershire sauce
Parmesan cheese
parsley

1. Heat the butter in the pan until it becomes brown but do not burn. Add the lemon juice, paprika, Worcestershire sauce and Parmesan cheese.
2. Brush each side of the fish with butter mixture and put on buttered foil and broil for about 10 minutes each side.
3. Serve with a sprinkle of parsley and more Parmesan.

Serves 4.

Sole with Mushrooms

4 fillets of sole	4 tablespoons wine
4 tablespoons (80 g) butter	½ cup scalded cream
salt and pepper	3 egg yolks, beaten
3 tablespoons grated onion	1 tablespoon parsley
12 oz (375 g) thinly sliced mushrooms	1 teaspoon lemon juice

1. Wash and dry the fish and grease a shallow baking dish.
2. Lightly salt and pepper the fish on both sides and lay them side by side on a buttered dish. Grate the onion over the fillets and add the mushrooms.
3. Pour over the wine and bake in a hot oven 400°F (200°C) for 12 minutes or until done.
4. Pour the scalded cream over the beaten egg yolks and season with salt and pepper, parsley and lemon juice.
5. Cook the sauce in a double boiler until it thickens. Do not boil. Make this sauce while the fish is cooking and try to have it finished when the fish comes from the oven. Pour it over the fish and serve immediately.

1½ lb (750 g) fillets of sole will serve 4.

Baked Snapper

3 lbs (1½ kg) snapper	Stock:
4 tablespoons parsley	bones of fish
2 tablespoons dill	1 sliced onion
½ cup (125 g) butter	salt and pepper
1 lemon, sliced	¾ cup (187½ ml) water
1 sliced onion	
salt and pepper	

1. Take out the backbone but leave on the head and tail of the fish.
2. Mix all the stock ingredients and simmer for 18 minutes.
3. Remove the bones from the stock but leave any residue of fish and onion.
4. Lay the fish in an oiled baking dish and fill the inside with dobs of butter, parsley and dill. Add salt and pepper and the broth.
5. Bake slowly 15 minutes per pound (30 minutes per 1 kg) basting occasionally.
6. Thicken the sauce with a little cornstarch and serve over the fish.

Cream may be added to the sauce for a richer taste.

Serves 4-6.

Chinese Fried Fish

1 large snapper
soya sauce
peanut oil
3 slices fresh ginger
3 chopped spring onions

salt and pepper
2 tablespoons sherry
½ cup (125 ml) water
cornstarch

1. Rub the fish with soya sauce on both sides and fry quickly in hot oil, 2 minutes each side.
2. Add the ginger, onions and a little salt, the sherry and water. Cover and simmer for about 10-15 minutes or until fish is done.
3. Dissolve a tablespoon of cornstarch in 3 tablespoons of cold water and add it a little at a time until the sauce thickens. Do not add it all unless it is needed.
4. Lift fish onto a hot platter and pour the sauce over it.

The fish may be steamed, and when done, onions sautéed in peanut oil and 2 tablespoons of soya sauce may be poured over it when ready to serve.

Serves 4-6.

Mexican Snapper

2 lb (1 kg) snapper fillets
batter and olive oil
   for frying
1 cup (250 ml) dry white wine
1 cup olive oil
1 cup vinegar
mustard

salt and pepper
1 onion, sliced
sweet gherkins
black and green olives
1 tablespoon capers
1 lemon
parsley

1. Cut the fillets into 1 inch (2½ cm) cubes and coat the fish in the batter and fry in olive oil. Let drain and cool.
2. Mix wine, olive oil and vinegar, dash of mustard, salt and pepper, sliced onion rings, gherkins (about 4 slices), olives, capers and juice of 1 lemon. Cover the fish and let stand in this marinade for about 2 hours at room temperature before serving.

Serve cold with either tartare, egg or mayonnaise sauce.

Serves 4.

Snapper Smoked Haddock and Mushrooms Scallops

2 tablespoons (40 g) butter
2 tablespoons cream
1 lb (500 g) cooked potatoes
8 oz (250 g) snapper fillets
8 oz (250 g) smoked haddock
2½ cups (600 ml) milk
2 tablespoons (40 g) butter
3 tablespoons flour
1 cup chopped mushrooms
salt and pepper
1 small can sweet corn
4 tomatoes
parsley

1. Mash the potatoes and blend the butter and cream in to make a smooth piping consistency (do not use all the butter and cream if it is not necessary).
2. Put the fish into the milk with about one third of the butter, simmer steadily until tender, about 12 minutes. Take the fish out, check for bones, and put aside on a plate to allow to cool.
3. Meanwhile heat the remaining butter in a pan, stir in the flour and cook for about 3 minutes, stirring all the time. Strain the milk used for the fish and mix slowly with the butter and flour mixture, bring to the boil and cook until smooth and thick.
4. Put in the mushrooms and cook for about 5 minutes. Add the flaked fish and corn. Season to taste.
5. Place in a shallow baking dish or individual ramekins and top with dobs of the mashed potato. Brown gently under the broiler. Garnish with tomato wedges and parsley before broiling if desired.

Serves 4-6.

Snapper Hungarian Style

2 lbs to 3 lbs (1 kg to 1½ kg) snapper
1 tablespoon (20 g) salt and pepper
12 mushrooms
sour cream
boiled potatoes

1. Leave the fish whole after cleaning and salt and pepper them inside and out and lay on a well oiled or buttered baking dish.
2. Make incisions to the bone 2 inches (5 cm) apart, placing sliced mushrooms in the incisions and around the fish.
3. Cover the fish with pieces of butter and ⅓ cup of sour cream.
4. Bake in a 350°F to 375°F (170°C to 190°C) oven for 30 minutes or until cooked through, basting regularly with butter and sour cream.
5. Five minutes before removing the fish from the oven add hot boiled, peeled and sliced potatoes around the fish, immersed halfway in the butter and sour cream.

Serves 4-6.

Baked Trout

fillets of trout	1 cup (250 ml) water
grated onion	¼ cup vinegar
parsley	3 peppercorns
lemon juice	1 clove
salt and pepper	1 bay leaf

1. Sprinkle fish with onion, parsley, lemon juice, pepper and salt and place in a buttered ovenproof dish.
2. Pour over water, vinegar, peppercorns, clove and bay leaf.
3. Cover with buttered paper and bake in a moderate oven for 15 minutes or until nearly cooked, remove paper.
4. Pour off liquid, strain, thicken and serve separately.

Trout can be whole, allow 20 minutes per 1 kg (10 minutes per pound).

Serves 4-6.

Baked Trout with Sardine Filling

2 lb (1 kg) boned trout
bacon strips
1 can sardines
1½ tablespoons flour
1 tablespoon white wine
   or lemon juice
1 tablespoon cream

Baste:
¼ cup (60 ml) white wine
¼ cup (cream)

2 egg yolks
salt and pepper

1. Bone and clean the trout.
2. Mash the sardines and blend in the flour and add the wine or lemon juice and the cream.
3. Season with salt and pepper and fill the fish and sew up.
4. Lay the fish on strips of bacon in a greased baking dish, first rubbing it with oil, salt and pepper.
5. Bake for 20 to 30 minutes according to the thickness of the fish.
6. Baste with the wine and cream and when done, remove the fish and add some of the sauce to the beaten egg yolks, return to oven for a moment then pour over fish. The sauce must be stirred well so it does not curdle.

Serves 4.

Fried Trout with Bacon

trout
mustard powder
salt and pepper
flour
bacon fat
garlic
lemon juice and parsley

1. Rub the trout with mustard powder and sprinkle the inside with salt and pepper.
2. Place flour, salt and pepper in a paper bag and put the fish inside and shake.
3. Melt the bacon fat with the crushed garlic and cook the fish in this until done.
4. Squeeze over lemon juice and garnish with bacon slices and a sprinkle of parsley.

Serves 4.

Poached Trout

whole trout, or fillets	4 peppercorns
½ cup chopped onions	1 bay leaf
½ cup chopped celery	2 teaspoons salt
½ cup chopped carrots	¼ teaspoon ginger
1 crushed clove garlic	¼ cup vinegar
2 tablespoons (40 g) butter	3 liters (3 quarts) water

1. Make the bouillon by cooking the onions, celery, carrots and garlic in the butter for 4 minutes without browning and adding all the other ingredients and boil for 5 minutes.
2. Lay the fish on a wire rack or in a basket and lower into the boiling bouillon. Simmer but do not boil. Allow 12 minutes per 1 kg (6 minutes a pound) for whole fish. Allow 20 minutes per 1 kg (10 minutes a pound) for fillets.

Serve with your favorite sauce. Hollandaise or Egg Sauce (see recipes) is suggested. Poaching takes much of the strong flavor from the fish and is a specially good method of preparing frozen trout which is often drier than fresh fish.

Serves 4.

Stuffed Trout

1 whole trout	1 small onion, chopped
1 cup (250 ml) sherry	1 tablespoon parsley, chopped
milk	½ teaspoon mixed herbs
salt and pepper	2 tablespoons (40 g) melted butter
Stuffing:	2 tablespoons hot water
1 cup white breadcrumbs	
salt	
pepper	

1. Wash and dry trout.
2. Place in greased casserole and pour sherry over, leave overnight.
3. Put stuffing into fish.
4. Add about 1 cup of milk, pepper and salt, to sherry and fish.
5. Bake for 10 minutes a pound (20 minutes 1 kg).

Serve hot or cold.

Serves 4.

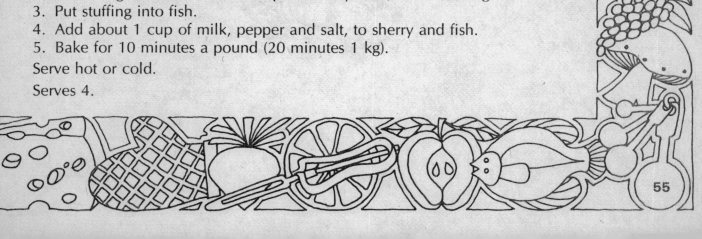

Trout with Almonds

1　fresh trout per person
4　tablespoons (80 g) butter
salt and freshly ground pepper
juice of 2 lemons
parsley
½　cup blanched sliced almonds

1. Rub trout with butter and sprinkle with freshly ground black pepper and pour over lemon juice. Place in a greased paper lined baking dish and bake in a hot oven for 10 minutes per pound (20 minutes per 1 kg).
2. Meanwhile melt the rest of the butter in a saucepan and add the almonds and cook until brown.
3. Serve pouring the butter and browned almonds over the trout and sprinkle with parsley.

Trout with Shrimp

4　portions trout, fillets
　　or whole
¾　cup (188 g) butter
1　cup shelled cooked shrimp
lemon juice
salt and pepper
parsley

1. Fry the fish in oil or butter in a pan. Do not let the butter burn. Remove the fish and set aside and keep warm.
2. In the same butter fry the mushrooms and shrimp for about 4 minutes and add the juice of at least 1 lemon together with salt and pepper to taste and some chopped parsley. Pour over the fish and serve.

Although this recipe is for trout any other kind of fish is suitable.

Serves 4.

Seafood Casserole

cooked fish	garlic
lobster	salt and pepper
shrimp	brown sugar
scallops	basil
oysters	milk
mussels	cream
peeled tomatoes	grated cheese
butter	parsley

1. Combine enough seafood in a casserole to cater for the required amount of people.
2. Stew at least 2 cups of chopped tomatoes in about 3 tablespoons (60 g) of butter with 1 clove of garlic, basil, salt and pepper and 1 teaspoon of brown sugar. Thicken the mixture with cornstarch and add equal milk and cream and stir until smooth.
3. Pour over the fish in a casserole and sprinkle with Parmesan cheese and parsley. Heat and brown in the oven.

The quantities are purely to taste and to the amount of people you are serving.

Baked Fish Parmesan

fish, whole or filleted
bacon strips
chopped parsley
olive oil
salt and pepper
crumbs
Parmesan cheese
lemon juice or white wine

1. Use either small fish, cleaned and boned, or fillets.
2. Rub the fish with olive oil or butter, salt and pepper.
3. Rub the fish into a mixture of fine crumbs and Parmesan cheese.
4. Place the fish on strips of bacon in a baking dish, add some lemon juice to the top or a little white wine.
5. Bake until the fish is tender. When done pour the sauce over the top and add a little more cheese if desired.

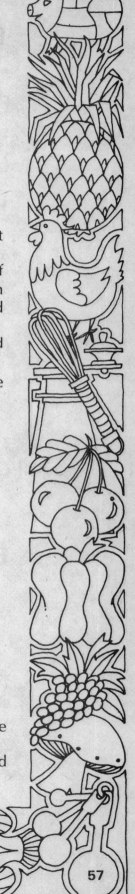

Baked Fish Russian Style

fish, whole or filleted
red or black caviar
1 egg, beaten
flour
salt and pepper
sour cream

1. One small fish or two fillets need 3 tablespoons caviar, 1 beaten egg, enough flour to hold the mixture together and seasoned with salt and pepper and a tablespoon of sour cream.
2. Fill the fish and sew it up or spread mixture in between two fillets and hold steady with skewers.
3. Bake slowly until fish is done.
4. Spread a little sour cream over the fish and sprinkle with Parmesan cheese.

Sliced mushrooms, sautéed, may be used in lieu of caviar.

Baked Fish with Anchovy Butter

fish fillets
½ cup (125 ml) soft butter
2 or 3 tablespoons anchovy paste
fine cracker crumbs
lemon juice
chopped parsley

1. Mix the butter and anchovy paste and spread the fillets with it inside and out.
2. Lay in a well greased baking dish, sprinkle with crumbs and bake until tender. Baste with a little water or white wine.
3. When done add lemon juice and chopped parsley.

Baked Fish with Chilli Sauce

fish, whole or filleted
2 tablespoons chilli sauce
1 tablespoon tomato sauce
½ cup sweet or sour cream
Parmesan cheese
chopped parsley

1. Skin fish by boiling it for several minutes in water and remove bones.
2. Mix the chilli and tomato sauce with cream and pour over the fish between the fillets.
3. Sprinkle with Parmesan cheese and bake slowly in a covered casserole.
4. Sprinkle with a little more Parmesan and chopped parsley.

Baked Fish with Sour Cream

3 lbs (1½ kg) fresh fish
strips of bacon
oil or butter
salt and pepper
1 cup sour cream
½ cup parmesan cheese
⅓ cup buttered crumbs
chopped parsley

1. Have the fish cleaned and well scaled. Rub inside and out with salt and pepper and oil or butter.
2. Lay the fish on several strips of bacon in the bottom of a baking dish.
3. Make a mixture of the cream, cheese, crumbs and lemon juice and spread it over the fish.
4. Bake in a moderate oven 350°F (180°C) until tender. Serve sprinkled with grated cheese and parsley.

Serves 4.

Baked Fish with Pernod

6 lb (3 kg) large white fish	2 tablespoons Pernod
6 medium onions, chopped	4 tablespoons olive oil
3 cloves garlic, crushed	1 large lemon, thinly sliced
4 tablespoons parsley	½ cup (125 g) butter, diced
150 ml (¼ pint) dry white wine	salt and freshly ground black
150 ml (¼ pint) water	pepper and tarragon

1. Combine the onions, parsley, dry white wine, water, Pernod and tarragon.
2. Put the fish into a large greased baking dish. Pour over a little olive oil.
3. Pour over the wine mixture and cover with thin slices of lemon. Dot with the butter and season with salt and pepper.
4. Bake in a hot oven 400°F (200°C) for 30 to 40 minutes or until done. Baste regularly. Add a little wine and water if fish becomes dry.

Serves 6.

Creamed Fish and Mushroom Quickee

fillets of any fine white
   fish (enough for 6)
1 pack dried cream of mushroom soup
½ cup breadcrumbs
¼ cup grated cheese

1. Poach fish in salted water until just tender. Drain, remove bones and leave in small pieces.
2. Make the mushroom soup according to directions on pack, and pour over the fish in an ovenware dish.
3. Mix breadcrumbs and grated cheese and sprinkle over.
4. Bake until top is browned and sauce bubbling.

Sautéed mushrooms can be added on top as a garnish.

Deep Fried Fish

2 lbs (1 kg) fish fillets
4 tablespoons flour seasoned
  with salt and pepper
2 eggs
2 tablespoons cold water

sufficient cooking oil to
  cover a heavy based
  frying pan to a depth of
  1½ inches (2 cm)

1. Cut fillets into serving pieces, after having washed fish and dried thoroughly.
2. Roll pieces of fish in seasoned flour.
3. Slightly beat egg and water with fork, and dip in fish pieces, thoroughly coating each fillet.
4. Heat oil in pan until a slight blue smoke appears. Arrange a few pieces of fish in the pan. Do not overcrowd the pan or overlap the pieces. Cook until golden brown.
5. Drain on brown paper.

Serve with Tartare Sauce (see recipe).

Fish in Their Jackets

1 lb (500 g) frozen puff
  pastry
6 small fillets of white
  fish
2 tablespoons (40 g) butter
¼ cup (30 g) flour
salt and pepper

5 oz (150 ml) milk
1 cup mushrooms
1 egg
1 tablespoon water
sliced lemon
parsley

1. Roll the pastry out thinly and cut into 6 squares, enough to cover the fish.
2. Lay the fillets out flat and season lightly. Make a thick sauce with the butter, flour and milk and add the chopped uncooked mushrooms and season well. Spread this over one half of each fillet. Fold the other half of the fish fillet over the sauce.
3. Lay on the square of the pastry, moisten the edges with a mixture of the egg and water, fold over in a triangle and seal the edges. Place on a baking sheet and brush with the egg and water mixture. Bake for 10 minutes in a hot oven at 475°F (240°C) just above the center, lower the heat and bake a further 25 minutes until brown and well risen.
4. Serve with lemon and parsley.

Flaked cooked fish can be added to the thick sauce and used as a filling for the pastry.

Serves 6.

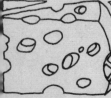

Fish Loaf

1 lb (500 g) cooked fish	2 teaspoons vinegar
2 cups (125 g) breadcrumbs	1 tablespoon lemon juice
1 egg	1 tablespoon anchovy paste
2 level tablespoons parsley, chopped	salt and pepper

1. Mix all ingredients together and bake for 1 hour.

This loaf may be steamed in a basin for 1½ hours or in small molds for ¾ hour.

Serve with a fish sauce.

Serves 4.

Fish Souffle

1 cup cold fresh or smoked fish	2 eggs
	lemon juice
1 cup well mashed potatoes	ginger
2 tablespoons (40 g) butter	parsley
2 tablespoons (40 ml) milk	salt and pepper

1. Place butter and milk over low heat, add potatoes and egg yolks and beat. Stir in fish and other ingredients. Mix well.
2. Fold in stiffly beaten egg whites.
3. Pour into a well greased oven dish with room for mixture to rise, and bake for 20 minutes.

Serve with a parsley sauce.

Serves 4.

Fish with Sour Cream

olive oil
fresh breadcrumbs
1 large onion
1 tablespoon (20 g) butter
4 fish fillets
fresh dill, chopped
   or 1 teaspoon dried dill

sour cream
chopped parsley
lemon juice
nutmeg

1. Brush a loaf tin with olive oil and sprinkle thickly with breadcrumbs.
2. Slice the onions and sauté in the butter until brown. Drain.
3. Put the fish fillets in layers alternately with onion slices, lemon juice, sour cream and nutmeg and bake in a moderate oven for 30 minutes or until the fish is done. Garnish with parsley and serve.

Serves 4.

Hawaiian Cutlets

4 portions of white fish
sliced cheese for each portion
½ cup sliced large shrimp
butter
lemon juice
pepper

1. Broil the fish brushing with butter or oil for at least 10 minutes each side.
2. Toss the shrimp in a little melted butter for 4 minutes, squeeze on one tablespoon lemon juice and a good shake of pepper.
3. Spoon over the top of the broiled fish and serve at once.

Garnish with wedges of lemon or more shrimp (unshelled).

Serves 4.

Malayan Fish

1 lb (500 g) fish (use boiling fish)
3 tablespoons (60 g) butter
½ cup flour
2 teaspoons curry powder
2 teaspoons chutney
3 slices pineapple, finely
   chopped

milk
½ cup cooked rice
salt
pepper
2 sliced hard-boiled eggs

1. Poach fish in a little water. Remove bones and flake the fish.
2. Reserve the fish stock.
3. Melt the butter, stir in the flour and mix well. Add the curry, chutney and pineapple. Gradually stir in the fish liquor with enough milk added to make 2½ cups (600 ml) liquid. Stir until it boils.
4. Add the flaked fish, rice, salt and pepper to taste and also some lemon juice. Fold in the sliced eggs.

Serves 4.

Stuffed Fish Mornay

2 lbs (1 kg) fish fillets
2 tablespoons finely
   chopped onion
2 tablespoons finely
   chopped celery
2 tablespoons bacon fat
1½ cups fine white
   breadcrumbs
½ teaspoon mixed herbs

1 tablespoon hot water
salt
pepper
1 tablespoon (20 g) butter
1½ tablespoons flour
1 cup (250 ml) milk
4 oz (125 g) grated cheese
salt and pepper
pinch mustard

1. Lay half of fish fillets in buttered baking dish.
2. Fry onion and celery in bacon fat. Add breadcrumbs, herbs, salt, pepper and hot water.
3. Spread this stuffing over the fish in the pan and cover with the remainder of the fish.
4. Melt the butter, add the flour, then the milk and stir until smooth and boiling. Add grated cheese, salt, pepper and mustard.
5. Pour over the fish and bake in covered dish at 350°F (180°C) for 45 minutes.

Extra sauce can be made and served separately.

Serves 4-6.

Piquant Fillets of Fish

1 lb (500 g) fish fillets
1 teaspoon paprika
1 tablespoon flour
½ teaspoon salt
pepper
1 beaten egg
½ cup cracker crumbs
⅓ cup (90 g) butter
2 tablespoons oil

1 teaspoon grated onion
½ cup (125 ml) water
1 tablespoon chopped parsley
1 chicken cube
3 tablespoons sherry
½ teaspoon thyme
dash pepper
1 cup (250 ml) sour cream

1. Dry fish thoroughly and dip in a seasoned flour, then in egg and finally in fine cracker crumbs.
2. Cook until golden brown in hot butter and oil and when cooked remove to a warm plate and make sauce.
3. To the fat remaining in the pan add grated onion, water, parsley, chicken cube, sherry, thyme and pepper. Bring to boil and remove from heat and add the sour cream. Return to heat and stir until hot.

Breadcrumbs may be used instead of cracker crumbs.

Serves 4.

Old English Fish

4 portions or whole fish
3 small onions, sliced
2 apples, chopped
1¼ cups (300 ml) cider
2 bay leaves
lemon

1. Sprinkle salt and pepper over the fish and put into a greased ovenproof dish.
2. Place all the onions and apples, over the top of the fish and pour over the cider and bay leaves.
3. Bake in a moderate oven 375°F (190°C) for about 30 minutes if fillets and 35 minutes if whole fish, or until done.

This dish is suitable for trout, whiting and mackerel.

Serves 4.

Fish Normandy

4 sole or whiting	2 tablespoons lemon juice
salt and pepper	sprinkle of cinnamon
¼ cup (30 g) flour	and nutmeg
3 tablespoons (60 g) butter	parsley
1 onion, finely chopped	Calvados or Chablis
3 apples, 2 chopped and 1 sliced	

1. Remove the heads from the fish and remove the backbone.
2. Season the flour and roll the fish in the seasoned flour.
3. Heat 2 tablespoons of the butter and fry the chopped apples and chopped onions until soft. Add lemon juice, cinnamon and nutmeg. Put aside and keep warm in a hot serving dish.
4. Heat the remaining butter in the frying pan and cook the fish until tender. Put on top of the apples and onions on the serving dish and garnish with apple slices and parsley, pour over 2 or 3 tablespoons of Calvados or Chablis.

Sole Milanaise

4 portions of sole or whiting	8 oz (250 g) flat noodles
salt and pepper	½ lb (250 g) button mushrooms
basil	1 cup cooked peas
3 tablespoons white wine	Parmesan cheese
2 tablespoons (40 g) butter	paprika
	lemon

1. Put the fish on a large plate and add the seasonings and about 2 teaspoons (10 g) butter. Place the plate over a pan of boiling water and cover with another plate or saucepan lid, if it fits, or cover it with foil. Keep the water boiling and allow to steam for 12 to 15 minutes.
2. Meanwhile boil the noodles in plenty of well seasoned water and saute the mushrooms in the remaining butter.
3. Drain the noodles and add to the mushrooms together with the peas. Heat gently for a few minutes. Put on a hot dish and lift the fish onto the noodles and garnish with Parmesan cheese, paprika and lemon to taste.

This is delicious served with any fish sauce.

Serves 4.

Skate with Capers

1 skate
water
3 tablespoons vinegar to each
   quart of water
1 large onion, sliced
mixture of herbs

bay leaf
salt and pepper
parsley, chopped
butter
2 tablespoons vinegar
2 teaspoons capers

1. Cut the skate into pieces and place in a pan and cover with water. Add vinegar, onion, mixed herbs and salt and pepper. Bring to boil and simmer for 80 minutes.
2. Remove the fish, take out any bones, skin and keep warm. Sprinkle parsley, salt and pepper over the fish.
3. Melt about 2 tablespoons (40 g) butter in a pan and when browned, but not burnt, pour it over the fish.
4. Meanwhile put the vinegar in a saucepan, add the capers and bring to boil and pour it over the fish.

This is nice served with boiled potatoes or rice and salad.

Serves 6.

Chablis Red Snapper

3 wine glasses of Chablis
1 tablespoon grated onion
1 tablespoon parsley
4 steaks of red snapper
salt and pepper

2 tablespoons (40 g) butter
canned sweet corn (1 small can
   creamed style)
Worcestershire sauce
Parmesan cheese

1. Place the fish in a mixture of the Chablis, onion and parsley and leave to marinate at room temperature for at least 1 hour.
2. Melt the butter and lift the fish out of the wine marinade and sprinkle with salt and pepper, brush the fish with the melted butter and broil for at least 10 minutes each side.
3. Meanwhile mix corn with a little Worcestershire sauce. Place fish in a long ovenproof serving dish and spoon over the sweetcorn mixture and sprinkle with Parmesan and parsley and pop under broiler until browned.

Serves 4.

Poached Fish with Wine

3 lbs (1½ kg) fresh fish	**Stock:**
½ cup (125 ml) fish stock	head, bones and skin
½ cup white wine	1 cup (250 ml) water
2 tablespoons (40 g) butter	1 thinly sliced onion
salt and pepper	salt and pepper
2 tablespoons flour	2 bay leaves
2 egg yolks, beaten	pinch thyme
½ cup heavy cream	½ teaspoon mace or nutmeg
	1 sliced carrot

1. Make the stock by adding all the fish trimmings with the rest of the stock ingredients and simmer for 30 minutes and strain.
2. Rub the fish with oil or butter, sprinkle with salt and pepper and lay in a pan, adding ½ cup strained stock and ½ cup white wine.
3. The fish may be cooked on top of the stove or in the oven.
4. Baste with the liquid until the fish is done.
5. Melt the butter in a saucepan and add the flour and when smooth blend in the sauce the fish cooked in.
6. Scald the cream, pour over the egg yolks and add it to the sauce. If necessary, thin to the right consistency with a little wine. Pour over the fish and serve. Garnish with slices of lemon and chopped parsley.

Serves 6-8.

Fish with Cashew Nuts

6 fish fillets	salt and pepper
2 teaspoons grated lemon rind	butter
2 tablespoons lemon juice	½ cup chopped cashew nuts
flour	parsley

1. Put the juice and rind of lemon in a shallow dish and allow the fish to stand in the mixture for at least 15 minutes.
2. Roll the fish in seasoned flour and fry in oil or butter until fish is tender.
3. Remove the fish, set aside and in the same pan fry and lightly brown the cashew nuts.
4. Serve the nuts over the fish and squeeze a little more lemon juice over the fish and sprinkle with a little parsley.

Serves 6.

Fish Caprice

6 large fish fillets
2 tablespoons flour
salt and pepper
1 egg, beaten
½ cup soft breadcrumbs

2 tablespoons grated
Parmesan cheese
2 medium sized bananas
sliced pineapple

1. Remove the skin from the fish and roll in the seasoned flour.
2. Dip the fish into the beaten egg and then coat in a mixture of the breadcrumbs and Parmesan cheese.
3. Fry in some butter or oil until done.
4. Peel the bananas and cut into halves lengthwise, drain the pineapple slices and fry them both gently in the pan until soft and golden brown.
5. Serve the fish with a slice of pineapple and banana on top of each fillet and sprinkle with parsley.

Serves 6.

Baked Fish Stuffed with Shrimp

3 lbs (1½ kg) fresh fish
8 or 10 shrimp, fresh, green
1 sliced onion
1 bay leaf
salt and pepper

1 egg, beaten
1 tablespoon flour
sherry
cream
Parmesan cheese

1. The fish can be small or it may weigh 2 lbs (1 kg) or more. It may be left whole or it may be boned and filleted. The quantity of stuffing depends on the number and size of fish.
2. Wash and cook the shrimp in ½ cup (125 ml) of water to which you have added the onion, bay leaf, salt and pepper. Strain and reserve the broth for baking the fish.
3. Peel the shrimp and grind or pound through a sieve or chop finely. Add the beaten egg, flour, and season with the sherry and cream, using only enough to make a soft stuffing. Season with salt and pepper.
4. Stuff the fish and either sew it up or use skewers. If stuffing fillets, lay dressing on top of one and cover with another, steadying them with a skewer.
5. Lay the fish on a strip of bacon, rub the top with a little oil and sprinkle with salt and pepper. Add a little broth and bake until done.
6. Sprinkle top with Parmesan cheese before taking from the oven. A little cream, a tablespoon of sherry and a little flour may be added to the sauce if desired.

Serves 4-6.

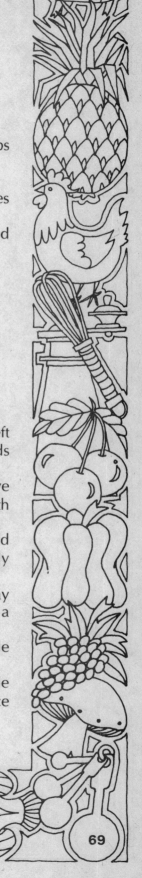

Fish Pie

2 lbs (1 kg) lobster tails
(shrimp or crabmeat), cooked
1 lb (500 g) fresh fish, snapper,
or flounder
1 lb (500 g) cooked shrimp
3 tablespoons (60 g) butter
4 tablespoons flour
1 cup (250 ml) fish stock
1 cup cream
mixed herbs

salt and pepper
3 tablespoons sherry
6 small white onions

Pastry:
1¼ cups flour
1 teaspoon salt
5 tablespoons (100 g) butter
or magarine
ice water

1. Cut the lobster tails into 1 inch (2½ cm) pieces. Shell the shrimp and put both aside.
2. Cook the fish in salted and herbed water for 30 minutes. Put aside to cool, remove fish and break up into good-sized pieces.
3. Boil the onions in very little water until just done. Add the onion water to the fish stock.
4. Arrange the fish in a baking dish with the onions, lobster and shrimp and make the sauce by melting the butter and mixing in the flour until smooth slowly adding the broth, the cream and the sherry.
5. Taste and season and pour over the fish.
6. Mix the ingredients for the pastry, roll out and cover the dish making incisions on the top for the steam to escape. Bake about 25 minutes in a moderately hot oven 375°F (190°C) or until the crust is brown.

Serves 6.

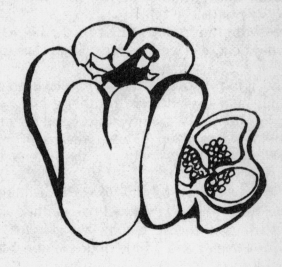

Creamed Smoked Haddock

enough smoked haddock
   for 4-6 people
1¼ cups (300 ml) milk
¾ cup cream
2 tablespoons (40 g) butter
2 hard-boiled eggs, chopped
salt and pepper
parsley

1. Cut the haddock into small pieces and put into a dish.
2. Warm the milk, cream, butter and add plenty of pepper.
3. Pour the mixture over the fish, cover and bake for about 25 minutes in a moderate oven 350°F (180°C).
4. Just before serving add the chopped hard-boiled eggs and sprinkle with parsley. Season to taste. The sauce may be thickened with a little corn-starch before you add the eggs.

Fish Pie Supreme

2 lbs (1 kg) cod
3 tablespoons (60 g) butter
5 tablespoons flour
3¾ cups (900 ml) milk
3 tablespoons grated cheese
salt and cayenne pepper
1½ cups uncooked rice
3 tablespoons (60 g) butter
1 small onion
1 tablespoon curry powder

1. Cook fish, drain and break into small pieces.
2. Melt butter, stir in flour, cook 3 minutes. Pour in milk and stir till smooth and thick, add cheese, salt and pepper. Simmer for 5 minutes with lid on.
3. Cook rice in salted water. Rinse in cold water to separate grains.
4. Melt butter in pan, fry onion, add rice, curry and salt. Stir constantly until rice is lightly browned. Pack into casserole, fill with cod and pour over cheese sauce. Place in oven to reheat when required.

A little soya sauce may be added before serving.
Serves 4-6.

Smoked Cod French Style

1 lb (500 g) smoked cod fillets	juice and grated peel of 1 lemon
2 cloves garlic, crushed	freshly ground black pepper
8 tablespoons double cream	toast fried in olive oil
¾ cup olive oil	or butter

1. Soak the cod fillets in cold water for at least 12 hours, changing the water often. Drain and place in a saucepan, cover with cold water and bring to the boil.
2. Remove from the heat, cover and let cod sit in the water for at least 7 minutes. Strain the fish, remove bones, skin and flake the fish.
3. Place the fish in an electric blender with crushed garlic, 3 tablespoons cream and 4 tablespoons olive oil and blend. Add the rest of the cream and olive oil alternately from time to time until the oil and cream are completely absorbed.
4. Put the mixture into a bowl over some hot but not boiling water, stir in lemon juice and peel and season to taste. Heat through and serve in a mound on a hot plate surrounded by fried toast squares.

This may also be served cold.

Serves 4.

Salmon and Green Pea Pie

1½ tablespoons (30 g) butter
1½ tablespoons flour
300 ml (½ pint) milk
salt and pepper, nutmeg
    and lemon juice
large thin salmon
small tin of peas
pastry

1. Make a sauce from the butter, flour, milk and seasonings. Add sufficient liquor from the tin of salmon and from the peas to make a smooth sauce. Boil 5 minutes.
2. Break salmon into pieces and stir through. Add the drained peas. Cool.
3. Line pie plate with the pastry, pour in the cold salmon mixture and cover with pastry and bake until golden brown.

Serves 4-6.

Salmon Royale

smoked salmon slices
cooked flaked whiting or
   similar fish
scallions or finely chopped
   small spring onions
grated rind of 1 lemon
chopped parsley

oil
white wine
juice of 1 lemon
fennel
artichoke hearts
capers
lemon slices

1. Season the slices of salmon with salt and pepper and spread with a thin layer of the flaked whiting, which has been mixed with the scallions and parsley.
2. Roll each into a good shape and secure with fine string.
3. Place rolls in a heavy pan side by side and pour over a small amount of oil. Spoon over a few tablespoons of white wine and lemon juice and sprinkle with the fennel and lemon rind.
4. Simmer very slowly with the lid on for 10 minutes.
5. Drain the rolls and place each on an artichoke heart on a serving dish. Moisten with some of the stock in which they have cooked and garnish with capers, lemon slices and parsley.

Serve with rice.

Serves 6.

Salmon Loaves

2 cups of flaked canned
   salmon or tuna
3 eggs, beaten
½ cup breadcrumbs
4 tablespoons (80 g) melted butter
½ cup (125 ml) Thick Cream Sauce
   (see recipe)

½ teaspoon baking powder
¼ teaspoon cayenne pepper
2 tablespoons lemon juice
1 tablespoon grated onion
1 tablespoon chopped parsley
salt and pepper
1 teaspoon grated lemon rind

1. Mix all ingredients together blending very well.
2. Pour the mixture into greased individual souffle dishes and bake in a moderate oven 350°F (180°C) for half an hour, placing the individual dishes in a pan of water.

Serve with hot mayonnaise with chopped pickle and capers added or Egg Sauce (see recipe).

Serves 6.

Salmon Scallops

1 lb (500 g) cooked flaked salmon (trout may be used)	½ cup (125 ml) milk
1 tablespoon (20 g) butter	chives
salt and pepper	parsley
2 tablespoons sherry	blanched almonds
2 eggs	breadcrumbs

1. Melt the butter and add cooked salmon. Season with salt and pepper.
2. Pour on sherry and simmer in saucepan with lid on for 10 minutes.
3. Beat eggs and add milk, salt and pepper to taste. Stir into fish adding chopped chives and chopped parsley.
4. Pour into scallop shells or oven dish. Top with breadcrumbs and sprinkle over with blanched sliced almonds.
5. Bake in moderate oven until set, about 15 minutes.

Serves 4.

Salmon Souffle

2 cups cooked salmon	½ cup cream
2 tablespoons ground parsley	salt and pepper
1 tablespoon ground onion	3 egg yolks beaten
2 tablespoons lemon juice	3 egg whites beaten separately

1. Flake the cooked salmon and add all the seasonings.
2. Add the beaten egg yolks and then fold in the stiffly beaten egg whites.
3. Place mixture into a greased casserole, set in a pan of cold water and bake in a moderate to slow 350°F (175°C) oven until set, about 20 minutes.

All types of cooked flaked fish may be used instead of salmon. Nice served with Tomato Sour Cream Sauce (see recipe).

Serves 4-6.

Steamed Salmon

1 thick slice of salmon
1 tablespoon onion juice
salt pepper
3 tablespoons lemon juice
2 tablespoons olive oil
  or butter
3 tablespoons capers
parsley

1. Rub the salmon with oil or butter.
2. Put the fish in baking dish with a tight lid. Pour over other seasonings.
3. Bake in a slow oven 325°F (165°C) oven about 30 minutes or until fish is done. Add 1 tablespoon of water if it becomes dry.

Nice served with brown or a light tomato sauce. This is a wonderful way to cook other fish which is not fat, rather than broiling.

Serves 4.

Curried Tuna Casserole

2 cups cooked macaroni, drained
1 can mushroom soup
2 cans tuna
1 chopped onion
2 tablespoons curry powder
2 tablespoons chopped parsley
½ cup sliced olives
1 large can tomatoes

3 sticks chopped celery
1 green pepper, chopped
salt
pepper
grated cheese
dry breadcrumbs
paprika

1. Mix all the ingredients together and place in a casserole.
2. Cover with dry breadcrumbs, grated cheese and paprika.
3. Bake for 1 hour at 350°F (180°C).

Serves 6-8.

Quick Tuna Souffle

3 eggs
1 can mushroom soup
1 can tuna
½ cup of whole kernel corn
1 tablespoon cheese, grated
basil
salt and pepper
2 tablespoons dry sherry

1. Separate the yolks and whites of eggs. Beat the whites until they are stiff.
2. Put the yolks of the eggs, which have been beaten, into a bowl with the soup, tuna, corn, cheese, basil, salt, pepper and sherry. Mix well. Fold in the egg whites.
3. Pour into a greased souffle dish and cook in preheated oven of 400°F (205°C) and reduce the heat to 350°F (180°C) and bake for 1 hour. Serve immediately.

Serves 4-6.

Tuna Fish Casserole

1½ cups tuna fish
1 cup mashed potato
2 tablespoons chopped parsley
2 tablespoons grated onion
1 cup (250 ml) milk
½ cup cream

2 tablespoons (40 g) butter
2 tablespoons flour
1 tablespoon lemon juice
salt and pepper
½ teaspoon curry powder

1. Drain the fish and flake it very finely.
2. Alternate layers of the fish and the potato in a greased baking dish, sprinkling each layer with a little onion and parsley and lemon juice.
3. Make a sauce by melting the butter, blending in the flour and slowly adding the milk, cream and seasonings. Pour it over the fish and bake about 20 minutes.

Grated cheese added to the top 10 minutes before the fish is cooked makes a nice addition.

Serves 6-8.

Crunchy Salmon Loaf with Creamy Sauce

1½ cups (375 ml) Sauce Base
3 cups (900 ml) water
salt and pepper
3 eggs
1 lb (500 g) can salmon or tuna
2 tablespoons finely chopped onion
1 teaspoon paprika
1 cup cooked rice

½ cup blanched almonds, split
1 sliced hard-boiled egg
parsley

Sauce Base:
2 cups skim milk powder
1 cup flour
1 cup (250 g) butter

1. Make the Sauce Base by rubbing the butter into the milk powder and flour until the mixture is like fine breadcrumbs.
2. Place the base in a saucepan and stir in cold water and seasonings.
3. Heat over low heat and stir until smooth. Pour half of sauce into a bowl. Cover remainder and put aside.
4. Separate egg yolks from whites and beat yolks well, add to the sauce bowl.
5. Add salmon, onions, paprika, rice and almonds.
6. Beat egg whites until stiff but not dry. Fold into the salmon mixture and turn into a well greased loaf pan.
7. Bake at 375°F (190°C) for 50 minutes. Unmold on a hot plate.
8. Meanwhile reheat reserved sauce over low heat and pour over loaf.
9. Garnish with slices of egg and parsley.

Serves 6-8.

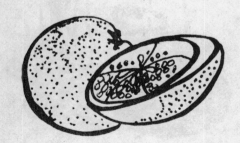

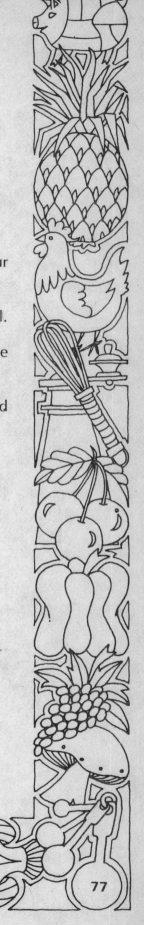

Sardine Pizza Pie

pie crust
4 large tomatoes
2 cans sardines
2 cups processed cheese
3 tablespoons chopped parsley
8 large stuffed olives
2 teaspoons Worcestershire sauce
salt and pepper
2 tablespoons flour

1. Line an 8 or 9 inch (20 cm or 23 cm) pie plate with pie crust having it slightly thicker than for a dessert pie shell. Prick and bake 10 minutes.
2. Drain sardines and arrange on the bottom of pastry shell. Add alternate layers of cheese, tomatoes, parsley, olives, onion, Worcestershire sauce, salt and pepper ending with cheese. Sprinkle each layer lightly with flour.
3. Arrange thin tomato slices petal fashion around outside of pie.
4. Reduce oven temperature to 350°F (170°C) and bake for 30 minutes.
5. Garnish with sliced olives and serve it immediately.

Serves 6.

Shellfish

Zucchini with Crabmeat

4 zucchinis about 6 inches (15 cm) long
1 tablespoon onion, grated
1 tablespoon (20 g) butter or oil
½ green pepper, chopped
1 large tomato, chopped and skinned
½ teaspoon basil
salt and pepper
1 tablespoon flour or cornstarch

1 cup (250 ml) dry white wine
soya sauce
mustard
parsley
2 cups crabmeat, canned, frozen or fresh
juice of 1 lemon
grated rind of 1 lemon

1. Cut the zucchinis lengthwise and scoop out the seeds leaving about 1 cm (½ inch) of flesh.
2. Cook zucchinis in a saucepan covering them with boiling water for 2 minutes.
3. Sauté onion in butter until soft, add green pepper, tomato, basil and seasoning and simmer 5 minutes. Thicken with flour or cornstarch and add wine and soya sauce.
4. Add the crabmeat and lemon juice and rind and heat through.
5. Put the mixture into the zucchinis and pop under a broiler to brown.

Serves 4.

Yvonne's Quick Crabmeat Dish

2½ cups flaked crabmeat, fresh or canned	½ teaspoon nutmeg
2 tablespoons grated onion	¼ cup sliced green pepper
3 tablespoons (60 g) butter	2 egg yolks, beaten
1¼ cups heavy cream	4 tablespoons sherry
1½ tablespoons flour	grated cheese
salt and pepper	crisp toast

1. Melt the butter in a frying pan, add the onion and cook gently for 1 minute.
2. Add the crabmeat and let it simmer for 2 minutes. Blend in the flour and when mixed, slowly add the cream and seasonings. Let cook 2 minutes and add the pepper which must be in fine slices and should be heated only.
3. Put some cream into the egg yolks and stir it into the crab but do not boil again.
4. Add sherry and serve immediately on slices of crisp toast, with sprinkled cheese.

This dish can be made at the table with a chafing dish.

Serves 6.

Crabmeat and Shrimp Peppers

1 large green pepper per person	paprika
½ lb (250 g) crabmeat or shrimp or a mixture of both	parsley
	Parmesan cheese
1 cup Thick Cream Sauce (see recipe)	

1. Cut the tops off the green peppers and seed them and pop into a saucepan and add water to about half the height of the peppers. Simmer in the covered pot for 3 minutes. Lift out and put aside. Be careful not to break them.
2. Meanwhile make the cream sauce, add the shrimp and crabmeat and season with salt, pepper and paprika to taste.
3. Carefully fill the peppers with the mixture and sprinkle with parsley and Parmesan cheese.
4. Cook in a moderate oven 350°F (180°C) for 20 minutes or until cooked.

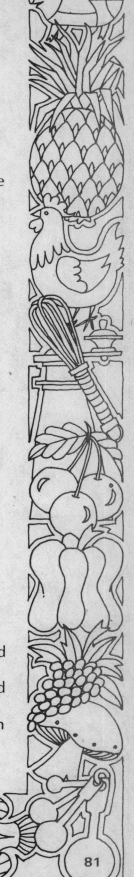

Crabmeat Burgers

1 cup flaked crabmeat,   salt and pepper
   cooked or canned   ½ teaspoon nutmeg
1 small beaten egg   cream
1 tablespoon grated onion   1 cup hot mashed boiled
1 tablespoon lemon juice   potatoes

1. Lightly mix all the ingredients, adding enough cream to make the mixture smooth, yet thick enough to form into cakes.
2. Sprinkle with breadcrumbs and chill.
3. Fry until light golden brown in either oil or butter.

These burgers can be made with chopped freshly cooked shrimp.

Serves 4-6.

Crabmeat Mornay

2 cups flaked crabmeat   ½ teaspoon nutmeg
2 tablespoons (40 g) butter   1 tablespoon lemon juice
½ cup (125 ml) white wine   1 cup sliced mushrooms,
2 tablespoons grated onion   sauteed
⅔ cup Thick Cream Sauce   1 cup grated Parmesan cheese
   (see recipe)

1. Place the flaked crabmeat in a pan with the butter, wine and onions and heat for 2 minutes.
2. Combine the cream sauce with the sliced, sauteed mushrooms and add the crabmeat, lemon juice and nutmeg.
3. Put into individual dishes or one large dish and sprinkle with Parmesan cheese. Cook until hot and place under the broiler to brown and serve.

Serves 6-8.

Quick Creamed Crab

1 lb (500 g) canned crabmeat	3 hard-boiled eggs, chopped
1 tablespoon (20 g) butter	½ cup celery, chopped
1 tablespoon Worcestershire sauce	1 dash tabasco
2 teaspoons grated onion	2 cups Thick Cream Sauce
1 small can mushrooms,	(see recipe)
button	1 wine glass dry sherry
1 teaspoon salt	grated cheese

Mix all the ingredients with Thick Cream Sauce. Add the wine and pour into a greased casserole. Sprinkle with cheese and bake in a moderate oven until sauce is bubbling and it is brown.

Serves 4-6.

Fried Shrimp with Herbs

butter
4 large green shrimp per
  person, shelled but leave
  on the tail
salt and pepper
parsley, chopped
fresh fennel
lemon juice

1. Melt enough butter in a pan to cover the bottom by about ½ inch (1 cm).
2. When the butter is bubbling toss in the shrimp and cook them for about 4 minutes on each side or until they are a good pink color.
3. Place the shrimp on individual ramekins and sprinkle with the salt, pepper, parsley, fennel and lemon juice.

Shrimp in Sour Cream

2 lbs (1 kg) small shrimp,
    cooked and shelled
¾ lb (375 g) button mushrooms
1 glass sherry
1½ cups sour cream
cayenne pepper
cornflour
large fluffy pastry shells

1. Slice the mushrooms and cook in some butter for 4 minutes. Toss the shrimp in and cook for 2 minutes.
2. Pour on the sherry and let stand for 1 hour to marinate.
3. Add sour cream, cayenne pepper and season to taste. Thicken with a little cornstarch and mix to a paste with a little more sherry if necessary.
4. Fill the pastry cases and heat in an oven for 15 minutes. Serve immediately while hot.

Serves 4-6.

Grilled Shrimp in Their Shells

enough large sized shrimp per
    person still in shells
oil
lemon
cayenne pepper

1. Lay the shrimp in their shells on foil on the grid of a broiling pan. Brush with oil and broil until the shells are golden brown.
2. Serve with lemon and cayenne pepper.

Live shrimp can be cooked this way instead of boiling them.

Shrimp Germaine

2 lbs (1 kg) shrimp	2 cups (500 ml) water
2 large onions	salt and pepper
4 garlic cloves	juice of 1 lemon
½ cup olive oil	1 sliced onion
3 tablespoons parsley	1 sliced carrot
1 teaspoon tomato purée	2 cloves garlic
salt and pepper	1 bay leaf
1 cup heavy cream	2 cloves
1 tablespoon flour	1 teaspoon basil

1. Wash the shrimp without peeling and place in the boiling mixture of water, salt and pepper, lemon juice, onion, carrot, garlic, bay leaf and basil. Cook gently for 10 minutes. Let the shrimp cool in the broth peel and set aside.
2. Chop the 2 onions and garlic very fine and cook in hot olive oil for 5 minutes. Do not brown. Add the chopped parsley and cook another 3 minutes. Add salt, pepper and tomato purée.
3. Add the shrimp and cook 5 minutes.
4. Just before serving add 1 cup of heavy cream mixed with the flour. Cook 2 minutes.

Serve with rice and green salad.

Serves 4-6.

Curried Lobster

1 medium onion, sliced	2 teaspoons brown sugar
1 medium apple, sliced	2 teaspoons coconut
2 tablespoons (40 g) butter	salt and pepper
2 teaspoons curry powder	1 heaped tablespoon flour
2 cups (500 ml) milk	juice of 1 lemon
2 teaspoons chutney	1 medium lobster
2 teaspoons raisins	chopped parsley

1. Sauté sliced onion and apple in melted butter with curry powder.
2. Add milk and other ingredients except flour.
3. When almost boiling, thicken with flour which has been mixed in a paste with a little milk.
4. Simmer 5 minutes.
5. Add chopped lobster meat, chopped into good sized pieces, parsley and lemon juice.

Serves 4.

Broiled Lobster

1 large cooked lobster
2 tablespoons (40 g)
   butter, melted
salt and pepper
lemon
parsley

1. Crack and devein the lobster and remove the flesh from the claws. Place the flesh on top of the body. Brush with the seasoned melted butter and squeeze over a few drops of lemon juice.
2. Broil until warmed through, basting all the time with melted butter and until the meat is golden browned.

Serves 2-4.

Lobster with Tomato Cream Sauce

1 lb (500 g) fresh lobster
4 tablespoons (80 g) butter
salt
1 tablespoon flour
¾ cup heavy cream
⅔ cup tomato sauce
freshly ground black pepper
1 teaspoon curry powder
1 jigger whiskey or brandy

1. Cut the cooked lobster into good sized pieces. Place in the top part of double boiler with the butter and heat for 3 minutes.
2. Sprinkle with salt and make the sauce by blending the flour with the cream, and cook a minute or two.
3. Add the pepper and curry powder to the tomato sauce and blend it with the cream. Cook for 2 minutes and let it stand at room temperature for 1 hour to bring out the flavor.
4. When ready to serve place lobster and butter in a heated serving dish, pour over the liquor and light for a minute.
5. Add the hot sauce. If this sauce is too thick add 1 or 2 tablespoons cream.

This is nice served with rice and green salad.
Serves 4.

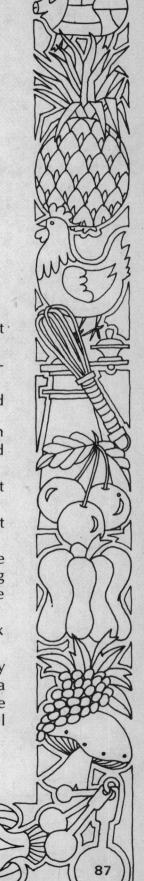

Lobster Souffle

3 1 lb (500 g) lobster, cooked
or 3 10 oz (350 g) lobster
tails cooked
¼ cup chopped carrots
½ cup chopped onion
1 tablespoon chopped parsley
1 tablespoon chopped chives
1 teaspoon paprika
1 cup heavy cream
½ cup sweet white wine
(sauterne)
3 tablespoons brandy

Sauce:
3 tablespoons (60 g) butter
3 tablespoons flour

1 cup milk
½ cup heavy cream
½ cup sherry

Souffle:
5 tablespoons (100 g) butter
6 tablespoons flour
salt and pepper
1½ cups milk
6 egg yolks, beaten
½ cup grated, Parmesan cheese
6 egg whites, room
temperature
½ teaspoon cream of
tartar

1. Cut the lobster meat into ½ inch (1 cm) thick pieces and set aside.
2. Saute the carrot, onion, parsley and chives in the oil until soft but not brown.
3. Toss in the lobster and add paprika, cream, wine and brandy. Cook gently, covered for 7 minutes.
4. Take out the lobster and reduce the cream mixture to 1 cup. Strain and set aside.
5. Meanwhile make the sauce by melting the butter in a saucepan, stir in the flour and beat until smooth and gradually add the milk, boil and remove from the heat. Add cream and sherry.
6. Add the 1 cup of the sauce with the lobster and pour into a 1¼ quart (1250 ml) souffle dish. Reserve the rest of the sauce.
7. Combine 1 cup of the sauce with the lobster and pour into a ¼ quart (1250 ml) souffle dish. Reserve the rest of the sauce.
8. Preheat the oven to 375°F (190°C) and make the souffle by melting the butter, stirring in flour, salt and cayenne pepper and gradually adding milk until smooth. Boil stirring all the time and then simmer until the sauce is thick.
9. Beat the mixture into egg yolks and mix well. Add the cheese and mix well again.
10. In a large bowl, beat egg whites with cream of tartar and salt until they are stiff. Fold the stiff egg whites into the egg yolks mixture a little at a time until it is well combined. Pour this over the lobster mixture in the souffle dish and bake in the oven for 35 to 40 minutes, or until well risen and golden brown.
11. Reheat the reserved lobster sauce and serve with the souffle.

Serves 6-8.

Lobster Thermidor

1 lb (500 g) lobster meat	dash Worcestershire sauce
2 tablespoons (40 g) butter	1 cup sliced mushrooms, sautéed
2 tablespoons flour	4 tablespoons sherry
1 cup cream	buttered crumbs
1 teaspoon mustard	Parmesan cheese
½ teaspoon nutmeg	
salt and pepper	

1. Make a cream sauce by melting the butter and adding the flour. Stir until smooth and slowly add the cream and cook for 2 minutes over a gentle flame.
2. Add the seasonings, mushrooms and lobster. Put the mixture into 4 or 5 shells and cover with buttered crumbs and cheese and broil them until golden brown.

If whole lobsters are prepared, first bake or broil them, remove the meat and cut into slices. Put a little cream sauce in the shells then the lobster meat, cover with the more sauce and top with crumbs and cheese and place under broiler.

Serves 4-6.

Seafood Kebabs

8 scallops	Marinade:
8 oz (250 g) bacon slices	6 tablespoons olive oil
8 large peeled shrimp	4 tablespoons dry white wine
chopped parsley	1 tablespoon honey
	nutmeg
	2 scallions, finely chopped

1. Separate the orange tongues from the scallops and cut white sections into half. Roll a small strip of bacon around each piece. Thread the rolls onto the skewers alternating with the peeled shrimp.
2. Place the marinade ingredients into a shallow dish and stand the kebabs in the mixture for at least 2 hours.
3. Cook gently under a grill for 10 minutes and sprinkle with finely chopped parsley, when ready to serve.

Serves 4.

Lobster Stew

1   lb (500 g) fresh lobster
    meat, cooked
4   tablespoons (80 g) butter
1   cup mushrooms, sautéed
1½ cups cream
2   eggs yolks
½   cup (125 ml) sherry
salt
pepper
¼   teaspoon mace or
    nutmeg
1   cup (250 ml) scalded milk

Court Bouillon or Stock:
2   cups (500 ml) water
1   large onion, sliced
1   bay leaf
sprig parsley
salt and pepper
pinch thyme
1   teaspoon tarragon
2   cloves garlic, crushed

1. Make the Court Bouillon or Stock by mixing all the ingredients and simmering for 20 minutes, strain and set aside.
2. Flake the cooked lobster in the top of a double boiler and heat for 5 minutes with the butter. Saute the finely sliced mushrooms in a little butter until tender about 6 minutes.
3. Add the mushrooms, bouillon and if it seems too thick, add the scalded milk.
4. When hot and ready to serve, scald the cream, pour it over the beaten egg yolks and add to the fish mixture. Add the sherry. Test for seasoning and serve.

Makes about 8 cups.

Lobster Pie

1 lb (500 g) cooked lobster
¾ lb (375 g) shrimp
½ lb (250 g) scallops
16 small white onions
mace
2 tablespoons (40 g) butter
2 tablespoons flour
1 cup cream
1½ cups (375 ml) shrimp
   broth and onion water
½ cup (125 ml) sherry

salt and pepper
½ teaspoon nutmeg
½ teaspoon paprika

Pastry:
1 cup (125 g) flour
⅓ cup (90 g) butter
½ teaspoon baking powder
½ teaspoon salt
ice water and milk

1. Cut the lobster into good sized pieces. Wash the shrimp, do not shell, and cook them in ½ cup (125 ml) water for 5 minutes.
2. Save the strained broth. Poach the scallops in it for 2 minutes.
3. Peel the shrimp.
4. Cook the onions in a little water until just done, drain and add this liquid to the shrimp broth. This should make 1½ cups.
5. Make the cream sauce of the butter, flour and all the seasonings, broth and cream. Arrange the fish in a big pie dish with the onions and add the sauce. Cover with pastry, made in the next step.
6. Cut the butter into the flour sifted with the salt and baking powder. Add just enough water and milk to wet it so it can be rolled and can cover the pie dish. Make incisions in the pastry to allow the steam to escape.

Creamed Mussels

1 lb (500 g) mussels	salt and pepper
1 cup (250 ml) water	2 tablespoons (40 g) flour
1 chopped onion	2 tablespoons (40 g) butter
1 sliced carrot	⅓ cup (84 ml) white wine
1 clove garlic, crushed	½ cup cream
1 bay leaf	2 beaten egg yolks

1. Clean the mussels thoroughly with a brush and steam over ⅓ cup of water less than a minute or until they open.
2. Remove from shells, catching all the juice and broth they have steamed over. Strain this and set aside.
3. In a cup of water place the onion, carrot, garlic, bay leaf, salt and pepper and boil for 15 minutes.
4. Make a cream sauce by melting the butter, stirring in the flour and adding the broth mixture.
5. Scald the cream and add it to the beaten egg yolks.
6. Combine this cream mixture with the broth and wine.
7. Heat and add the mussels and serve over crisp hot toast.

This is an excellent sauce served over fish.

Serves 4.

French Fried Shellfish

oysters, mussels or shrimp
4 beaten eggs
4 tablespoons flour
salt and pepper
oil

1. Peel and split and remove the veins from shrimp.
2. Beat the flour and eggs together and add salt and pepper.
3. Dip the raw fish into the batter and fry 30 seconds to a minute in deep hot oil to a golden brown. Shrimp could take a little longer.
4. Drain on brown paper and serve immediately.

Serve with Tartare Sauce (see recipe).

Shrimp with Garlic and Wine Sauce

1 lb (500 g) large shrimp	salt and pepper
5 cloves of crushed garlic	3 tablespoons vermouth or
5 tablespoons olive oil	white wine
2 tablespoons chopped parsley	Parmesan cheese

1. Peel and de-vein the shrimp. Rinse quickly under running water.
2. Heat the oil and sauté the garlic for about two minutes.
3. Add the shrimp and parsley and cook gently on both sides for about five minutes. Season with salt and freshly ground pepper.
4. Add the wine and stir well. Serve on hot plates. Sprinkle with Parmesan cheese.

Serves 4.

Scallops in Wine

enough scallops for 4 people
2 tablespoons (40 g) butter
1¼ cups (300 ml) white wine
salt and pepper
1½ cups white breadcrumbs
2 tablespoons (40 g) butter
parsley

1. Heat 2 tablespoons butter in a large pan and toss the scallops in this for about 2 minutes, add the wine and seasoning.
2. Simmer for 4 minutes or until just tender.
3. Meanwhile toss the breadcrumbs in 2 tablespoons melted butter and when crisp place the crumbs in a pie dish or individual dishes and top with the cooked scallops. Garnish with parsley and serve.

Lobster Newburg

2½ cups cooked fresh lobster
4 tablespoons (80 g) butter
1 tablespoon flour
salt and pepper
½ teaspoon flour

salt and pepper
½ teaspoon nutmeg
1¾ cups heavy cream, scalded
3 egg yolks, beaten
½ cup (125 ml) sherry or Madeira

1. Melt the butter in the top part of a double boiler and let the lobster warm in it for 3 minutes.
2. Blend in the flour until smooth. Add the seasonings and the scalded cream which has been mixed with the egg yolks. Stir until it thickens a little.
3. Add the wine and serve immediately.

This may be served on hot crisp toast or in patty or pastry shells. Brandy can be used instead of sherry or Madeira but if doing so use a little less.

Serves 4-6.

Oyster Pie

2 tablespoons (40 g) butter
2½ tablespoons flour
1½ cups (375 ml) cold milk
¼ cup oyster liquor
salt and pepper
nutmeg, thyme and cayenne
    to taste
lemon juice
2 dozens small oysters
pastry

1. Make a sauce in the usual way with butter, flour, milk, oyster liquor and seasonings. Cool and add a little lemon juice.
2. Place an equal amount of sauce mixture in individual dishes, with 6 oysters on the top of each and then cover with another layer of sauce.
3. Roll out pastry; adjust on top of each dish and make a few slits in the crusts to allow steam to escape.
4. Bake in very hot oven 450°F (230°C) until golden brown.

Serves 4-6.

Fresh Water Shrimp

fresh water shrimp (large)
butter
lemon juice
garlic
salt and pepper

1. Fresh water shrimp are often available from the local fish shop or from your main fish markets. If they are not already cooked for you, place fresh shrimp in a large saucepan of boiling water for approximately 10-15 minutes.
2. Crush the garlic and add to the butter, add lemon juice, salt and pepper and melt together and cook for 2 minutes.
3. Serve warm in a bowl together with hot french loaves of bread.

Index

Lobster Thermidor 88
Lobster with tomato cream sauce 86

Malayan fish 64
Mango and lobster salad 28
Mayonnaise cream sauce for lobster 41
Mexican snapper 51
Mornay sauce 36
Mushrooms with crabmeat 19
Mushrooms and tomato stuffings 42

Oil mayonnaise 41
Old English fish 65
Oysters au gratin 21
Oyster bisque 22
Oyster pie 93
Oyster Rockefeller 22
Oyster soup 10

Pancakes with caviar 18
Parmesan and mayonnaise sauce for fish 42
Pineapple and shrimp salad 26
Piquant fillets of fish 65
Poached fish with wine 68
Poached trout 55

Quick creamed crabs 82
Quick tuna souffle 76

Ravigote sauce for mussels or clams 35

Salmon and green pea pie 72
Salmon Royale 73
Salmon loaves 73
Salmon rice salad 24
Salmon ring 23
Salmon scallops 74
Salmon souffle 74
Sardine pizza pie 78
Savory snapper 49
Seafood casserole 57
Seafood kebabs 88
Shrimp bisque 16
Shrimp Germaine 84
Shrimp mousse 27
Shrimp pancakes 20
Shrimp Remoulade 29
Shrimp sauce 36
Shrimp Southern style 29

Shrimp in sour cream 83
Shrimp with garlic and wine sauce 92
Skate with capers 67
Smoked oyster soup 11
Smoked salmon pate 17
Smoked salmon rolls 17
Smoked cod French style 72
Snapper Hungarian style 53
Snapper, smoked haddock
   and mushrooms scallops 52
Sole and lemon 46
Sole French style 47
Sole Milanaise 66
Sole Normandie 48
Sole Scandinavian 44
Sole with grapes 47
Sole with mushrooms 50
Sour cream mayonnaise 42
Southern style crab 28
Steamed salmon 75
Stuffed fish mornay 64
Stuffed whiting 49
Stuffed trout 55

Taramasalata 15
Tartare sauce 35
Tasmanian scallops in wine 92
Thick cream sauce 34
Tomato and cheese sauce 34
Tomato sour cream sauce 34
Trout with almonds 56
Trout with shrimp 56
Tuna fish casserole 76
Tuna salad Spanish style 24

Veloute sauce 33

Whiting in aspic 26
Whiting in tomato and wine sauce 45

Yvonnes quick crabmeat dish 80

Zucchini with crabmeat 79

8000-4-S65